AAT

Certificate in Accounting

Principles of Bookkeeping Controls

Course Book

For assessments from September 2023

Sixth edition 2023

ISBN 9781 0355 0586 9

Previous ISBN 9781 5097 4384 1

ISBN (for internal use only) 9781 0355 0487 9

eISBN 9781 0355 0446 6

British Library Cataloguing-in-Publication Data

A catalogue record for this book is available from the British Library

Published by

BPP Learning Media Ltd

BPP House, Aldine Place

142-144 Uxbridge Road

London W12 8AA

www.learningmedia.bpp.com

Printed in the United Kingdom

Your learning materials, published by BPP Learning Media Ltd, are printed on paper obtained from traceable sustainable sources.

Contains public sector information licensed under the Open Government Licence v3.0

A note about copyright

Contents

Introduction to the course

Syllabus overview

This unit builds on the knowledge and skills acquired from studying *Introduction to Bookkeeping* and explores control accounts, journals and reconciliations. It takes students through a number of processes used in bookkeeping that help verify and validate the entries made. These processes enable the student to understand the purpose of control accounts and associated reconciliations. Students will also understand the use of the journal to the stage of redrafting the trial balance, following initial adjustments.

(AAT Qualification Specification, Version 4.0 published January 2023, page 41)

Assessment method	Marking type	Duration of assessment
Computer-based unit assessment	Computer marked	1 hour 30 minutes

Learning outcomes	Weighting
Use control accounts	25%
Reconcile a bank statement with the cash book	25%
Use the journal	25%
Produce trial balance	25%
Total	**100%**

Assessment structure

1.5 hours duration

Competency is 70%

Note. This is only a guideline as to what might come up. The format and content of each task may vary from what is listed below.

Your assessment will consist of 8 tasks.

Task	Expected content	Max marks	Chapter ref	Study complete
Task 1	**Control accounts** This task will test your knowledge of control accounts. It may include questions on the receivables, payables and VAT control accounts. You may be asked to complete a control account and/or calculate the closing balance. There will also be short, factual questions which test your knowledge of this topic.	10	(3) Introduction to control accounts	

Task	Expected content	Max marks	Chapter ref	Study complete
Task 2	**Control accounts** This task is about reconciling control accounts. You may be asked to identify differences between the control account and its related ledger account, and explain likely reasons for the difference.	10	(3) Introduction to control accounts and (4) Preparing and reconciling control accounts	
Task 3	**Payment methods and bank reconciliations** This task is about payment methods and reconciling the cash book to the bank statement. You will be asked to show your understanding of the different payment methods available to businesses. You may also be asked to demonstrate your knowledge of bank reconciliations through a series of objective-test questions.	8	(1) Payment methods and (2) Bank reconciliations	
Task 4	**Payment methods and bank reconciliations** This task is about reconciling a bank statement with the cash book. You may be asked to update a cash book and complete a bank reconciliation statement.	12	(1) Payment methods and (2) Bank reconciliations	
Task 5	**The journal** This task is about using the journal. You will be asked to demonstrate your knowledge of the journal and make postings to the nominal (general) ledger. Having processed transactions through the journal, you may also be asked to calculate the closing balance on an account.	10	(5) The journal	
Task 6	**The journal** This task is about using the journal to correct journals. You will be asked to identify and correct errors using the journal. You may be asked to clear a suspense account balance and also show whether different types of errors are likely to be identified through the trial balance.	10	(5) The journal and (7) Errors and the trial balance	

Task	Expected content	Max marks	Chapter ref	Study complete
Task 7	**Trial balance** This task is about extracting a trial balance. You will need to balance off ledger accounts and, having balanced them off, the closing balances can be transferred to the trial balance. To complete the task you may need to total the trial balance.	10	(6) Initial trial balance	
Task 8	**Re-drafting the trial balance** This task is about re-drafting a trial balance. You will be given an initial list of balances and also journals to process. You will include the adjusted balances in the trial balance and, if required, enter totals for the debit and credit columns.	10	(7) Errors and the trial balance	

Skills bank

Our experience of preparing students for this type of assessment suggests that to obtain competency, you will need to develop a number of key skills.

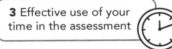

What do I need to know to do well in the assessment?

Principles of Bookkeeping Controls is the second of the two mandatory financial accounting assessments at Level 2. It is designed to build on your knowledge of double entry and the other topics introduced in *Introduction to Bookkeeping*.

To be successful in the assessment you need to:

- Understand the different payment methods and the effect these methods have on the bank balance
- Identify the most appropriate payment method and the features of the main payment methods
- Update the cash book and perform a bank reconciliation
- Prepare control accounts and reconcile the control accounts with the related ledger
- Process adjustments using the journal
- Produce and redraft the trial balance following adjustments.

Assumed knowledge

The following topics were studied in *Introduction to Bookkeeping* and are also relevant to this assessment:

- **Double entry bookkeeping** – *Principles of Bookkeeping Controls* is still largely a test of your double entry skills, although at this level, new accounting entries are introduced, such as payroll journals. This means it is vital that you are comfortable with the double entry studied at *Introduction to Bookkeeping* before we build on this knowledge.

- **Control accounts** – the receivables ledger, payables ledger and VAT control accounts were introduced in *Introduction to Bookkeeping*. They are studied in more detail in *Principles of Bookkeeping Controls*, where control account reconciliations are also examined.

You can see that several topics that were introduced in *Introduction to Bookkeeping* that are now studied in more depth at *Principles of Bookkeeping Controls*. The most important thing to do, though, is to consolidate your understanding of double entry bookkeeping before your *Principles of Bookkeeping Controls* course starts.

Assessment style

In the assessment you will complete tasks by:

(a) Entering your answer by selecting from drop down menus of options known as **picklists**

(b) Using **drag and drop** menus to enter your answer

(c) Typing in numbers, known as **gapfill** entry

(d) Entering **ticks**

(e) Entering **dates** by selecting from a calendar

You must familiarise yourself with the style of the online questions and the AAT software before taking the assessment. As part of your revision, log in to the **AAT website** and attempt their **online practice assessments**.

Introduction to the assessment

The question practice you do will prepare you for the format of tasks you will see in the *Principles of Bookkeeping Controls* assessment. It is also useful to familiarise yourself with the introductory information you **may** be given at the start of the assessment. For example:

You have **1 hour and 30 minutes** to complete this assessment.

- This assessment contains **8 tasks** and you should attempt to complete **every** task.

- Each task is independent. You will not need to refer to your answers to previous tasks.

- The total number of marks for this assessment is 80.

- Read every task carefully to make sure you understand what is required.

- Where the date is relevant, it is given in the task data.

- Both minus signs and brackets can be used to indicate negative numbers **unless** task instructions state otherwise.

- You must use a full stop to indicate a decimal point. For example, write 100.57 **not** 100,57 or 10057.

- You may use a comma to indicate a number in the thousands, but you don't have to. For example, 10000 and 10,000 are both acceptable.

- Mathematical rounding should be applied where appropriate.

(a) As you revise, use the **BPP Passcards** to consolidate your knowledge. They are a pocket-sized revision tool, perfect for packing in that last-minute revision.

(b) Attempt as many tasks as possible in the **Question Bank**. There are plenty of assessment-style tasks which are excellent preparation for the real assessment.

(c) Always **check** through your own answers as you will in the real assessment, before looking at the solutions in the back of the Question Bank.

Key to icons

Key term

A key definition which is important to be aware of for the assessment.

Formula to learn

A formula you will need to learn as it will not be provided in the assessment.

Formula provided

A formula which is provided within the assessment and generally available as a pop-up on screen.

Activity

An example which allows you to apply your knowledge to the technique covered in the Course Book. The solution is provided at the end of the chapter.

Illustration

A worked example which can be used to review and see how an assessment question could be answered.

Assessment focus point

A high priority point for the assessment.

Open book reference

Where use of an open book will be allowed for the assessment.

Real life examples

A practical real life scenario.

AAT qualifications

The material in this book may support the following AAT qualifications:

AAT Foundation Certificate in Accounting Level 2, AAT Foundation Certificate in Accounting at SCQF Level 5 and Certificate: Accounting Technician (Level 3 AATSA).

Supplements

From time to time we may need to publish supplementary materials to one of our titles. This can be for a variety of reasons, from a small change in the AAT unit guidance to new legislation coming into effect between editions.

You should check our supplements page regularly for anything that may affect your learning materials. All supplements are available free of charge on our supplements page on our website at:www.bpp.com/learning-media/about/students

Improving material and removing errors

BPP Learning Media do everything possible to ensure the material is accurate and up to date when sending to print. In the event that any errors are found after the print date, they are uploaded to the following website: www.bpp.com/learningmedia/Errata

These learning materials are based on the qualification specification released by the AAT in January 2023.

BPP

1 Payment methods

Learning outcomes

2	Reconcile a bank statement with the cash book
2.1	**Payment methods**
2.1.1	Learners need to understand: different payment methods:

different payment methods:

- cash
- cheque
- debit card
- credit card
- bank draft
- standing order
- direct debit
- BACS (Bankers' Automated Clearing Services)
- direct credit
- CHAPS (Clearing House Automated Payment System)
- Faster Payments

2.1.2	that different payment methods affect the bank balance in different ways:

- reduce funds on the date of payment
- reduce funds at a later date
- have no effect.

Assessment context

The assessment will test your understanding of the main payment methods available to businesses. You will also need to understand how these different payment methods affect the bank balance.

Qualification context

Payment methods are only examined in this unit. However, this topic provides useful background knowledge for the other units in the qualification.

Business context

All modern businesses use at least some of the many services offered by banks. In order to determine the most appropriate method of payment it is important to understand the effect payment methods have on the bank balance.

Chapter overview

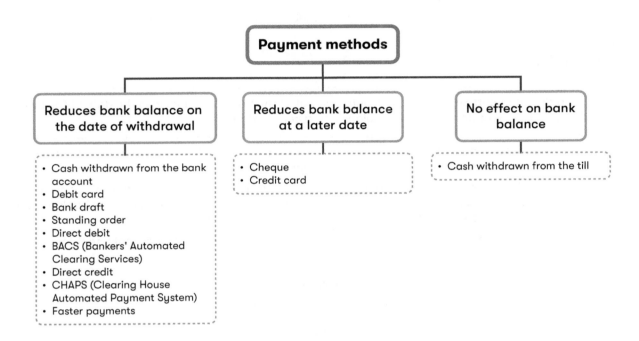

Payment methods

Reduces bank balance on the date of withdrawal

- Cash withdrawn from the bank account
- Debit card
- Bank draft
- Standing order
- Direct debit
- BACS (Bankers' Automated Clearing Services)
- Direct credit
- CHAPS (Clearing House Automated Payment System)
- Faster payments

Reduces bank balance at a later date

- Cheque
- Credit card

No effect on bank balance

- Cash withdrawn from the till

Introduction

Cash flow is crucial to a business's survival and if a business is to run efficiently, it must:

(a) Understand the different payment methods available to settle transactions

(b) Appreciate the effect different payment methods have on the bank balance

1 Banks

> **Bank statement:** Shows payments into and out of the bank account since the date of the last bank statement and the closing balance on a certain date.

Businesses must ensure that money received from customers and other sources is paid into a bank account, so that the bank can hold and safeguard the money for them.

At regular intervals, a business's bank will send out a **bank statement** showing transactions on the bank account since the date of the last bank statement, and a final balance on the bank account. Many businesses also view their transactions and balances online.

You will be familiar with bank statements; however, it is useful to see a bank statement for a typical business:

First National

11 High Street, Greenfield, GR5 2LL

To: Jones & Co   **Account number:** 38291035   22 October 20XX

20XX	Details	Paid out £	Paid in £	Balance £
17 Oct	Balance brought forward			1,595.23 C
18 Oct	Cheque no 003067	424.80		
	Cheque no 003069	122.60		1,047.83 C
19 Oct	DD Benham District Council	450.00		
	Transfer		1,081.23	1,679.06 C
20 Oct	Cheque no 003073	1,480.20		
	Cheque no 003074	1,865.67		1,666.81 D
21 Oct	Transfer		1,116.20	550.61 D
	Balance carried forward			550.61 D

You may have noticed something strange about the debit and credit terminology related to the daily balances on the bank statement.

- A positive balance on the account is shown as a credit.
- An overdraft balance is shown as a debit.

This is the opposite way round to the way in which debits and credits are treated in the bank account in the organisation's own books – money held by the business is a debit balance and an overdraft is a credit balance!

2 Payment methods

The main payment methods available to businesses are:

- Cash
- Cheque
- Debit card
- Credit card
- Bank draft
- Standing order
- Direct debit
- BACS (Bankers' Automated Clearing Services)
- Direct credit
- CHAPS (Clearing House Automated Payment System)
- Faster payments

> **Assessment focus point**
>
> In the assessment you need to demonstrate knowledge of the different types of payment method by selecting the most appropriate method in a particular scenario. You will also be asked to show the impact the payment methods have on a business's bank balance.

2.1 Cash

Owing to the rise in electronic transactions, cash is becoming a less common method of payment for businesses. However, it is still used for low-value transactions.

If a business receives cash from customers, it must be counted before it can be banked. You need to determine how many of each type of coin or note you have, the value of each type and the total value.

The easiest way to do this is to make piles of coins or notes to a set value, say £5 or £1.

> **Paying-in slip:** A pre-printed document for paying cash and cheques into a bank account.

Example: Paying-in slip (paying coins and notes into the bank)

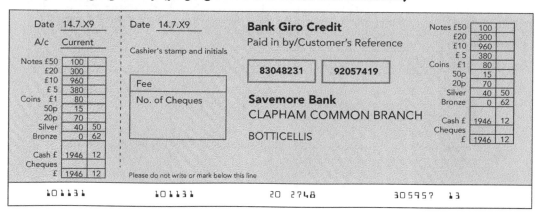

When cash is paid into the bank account (using a **paying-in slip**) it will appear as a '**counter credit**' on the bank statement of the business receiving the money.

Effect of cash payments on the bank balance

When cash is withdrawn from the bank account, the bank balance is immediately reduced by the amount withdrawn.

However, if a payment is made from the cash till this will have no effect on the bank balance as the money is not in the bank account at the point the transaction occurs.

2.2 Cheques

> **Cheque:** A customer's written order to their bank to pay a specified sum to a particular individual/organisation.

Cheques are a reasonably common method of payment. They are a written order to the bank, signed by the bank's customer to pay a certain amount to another person or company.

There are three parties involved in a cheque:

Name	Detail
Drawee	The bank that has issued the cheque and will have to pay the cheque
Payee	The person to whom the cheque is being paid (eg the supplier)
Drawer	The person who is writing and signing the cheque in order to make a payment (eg the customer)

When a cheque is prepared, the following details must be included:

- Name of **payee**
- Amount in words and figures
- Date
- Signature of an authorised person

Example: Cheque

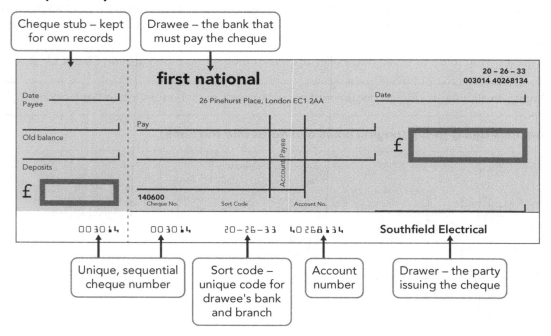

> **Clearing system:** The system set up by the major banks to deal with the payment of cheques which means there is typically a delay of three business days between paying a cheque into an account and being able to access the money.

If you write out a cheque, then the eventual outcome is that the money will be paid out of your bank account and into the account of the payee of the cheque. The cheque must be banked by the payee and then clear into their account before the money is available for use. The **clearing system** is used for this process.

Generally, it takes around three working days for a cheque paid into a bank account to clear into that account. At this point, the funds can be drawn on by the recipient of the cheque.

When cheques are paid into a bank account (using a paying-in slip) they will appear as a 'counter credit' on the bank statement of the business receiving the money.

2.2.1 Dishonoured cheques

> **Dishonoured cheque:** A cheque that has not been paid as expected by the bank on which it is drawn.

Some cheques may be dishonoured by the **drawee** because, for example, there are insufficient funds in the **drawer**'s account. A **dishonoured cheque** is sent back to the payee so that payment can be pursued in some other way.

Effect of cheque payments on the bank balance

The payer's bank balance is reduced after the date of payment.

2.3 Debit card

> **Debit card:** A card that allows the customer to purchase goods and services where the sale is automatically debited from the customer's bank account and credited to the supplier's bank account.

A **debit card** is an electronic payment card that allows you to make transactions in person and remotely (by telephone and online). It takes payment directly from your bank account.

When a debit card is used to pay for a transaction, the amount of the sale is automatically debited from the customer's bank account and credited to the retailer's bank account.

There is no need to pay debit card 'receipts' into the bank as this is done at the point of sale.

Effect of debit card payments on the bank balance

A debit card payment reduces the payer's bank balance immediately.

2.4 Credit card

> **Credit card:** A card that allows the customer to purchase goods and services on credit now but gives them flexibility as to when they repay the credit card company.

Credit cards are another common method of payment. A business can pay for goods and services by credit card at outlets that accept credit card payments.

The business is sent a credit card statement every month showing:

- All of the purchases on the credit card since the previous statement
- The total outstanding on the credit card
- The minimum payment required
- The date by which payment should reach the credit card company

The customer can then choose whether to pay off the full amount outstanding on the account or only part of it. Any unpaid outstanding amount will have interest charged on it, which will appear on the next credit card statement.

Effect of credit card payments on the bank balance

A credit card payment will not affect the payer's bank balance until the amount outstanding on the credit card is settled. Therefore, purchases do not have an immediate effect on the bank balance.

Activity 1: Effect payment methods have on the bank balance (part 1)

Identify the effect the different payment methods have on the bank balance.

Payment method	Reduce funds on the date of payment ✓	Reduce funds at a later date ✓
Cash withdrawal from bank account		
Cheque		
Debit card		
Credit card		

2.5 Bank draft

A **bank draft** is a non-cancellable cheque drawn on the bank rather than the customer's account.

The business will request a bank draft specifying the payee and the amount.

The bank will then take this amount (plus a fee) from the business's bank account and provide the bank draft. The bank draft will be sent to the supplier.

Payment via a bank draft is guaranteed and is usually used for large payments, especially where payment is overseas or in a foreign currency.

Effect of bank draft payments on the bank balance

Once the bank agrees to issue the bank draft, the individual/business making the payment must immediately transfer the amount of the draft (plus any applicable fees and charges) from their own account to the bank's account. Therefore, the bank balance is reduced at that point.

2.6 Standing order

> **Standing order:** A method of making the same regular payment directly from a business's bank account to the bank account of a supplier or other third party.

A **standing order** is used to make the same regular payment directly from a business's bank account to the bank account of a supplier or other third party. This is organised through the bank by filling in a standing order schedule (either paper or online).

Standing orders enable a business to make regular payments to the bank account of a third party. The standing order will be for a fixed amount.

Example: Standing order schedule

Standing order schedule		
To		
Please make the payments as detailed below and debit my account:		
Name of account to be debited		
Account number		
Payee details		
Name of payee		
Bank of payee		
Sort code of payee		
Account number of payee		
Amount of payment (in words)		£
Date of first payment		
Frequency of payment		
Continue payments until		
Signature		Date

Effect of standing orders on the bank balance

Payment by standing order reduces the payer's bank balance on the date the payment is made.

2.7 Direct debit

> **Direct debit:** A method of making payments direct from the bank where payments are for variable amounts and/or varying time intervals.

Direct debit is also a method of making a payment directly from the business's bank account to that of another party. However, with a direct debit payment:

(a) The receiver initiates the payment and chooses the amount of each payment

(b) The payments can vary in amount

As the payments can vary in amount, it is useful for regular, variable expenses such as telephone expenses.

To set up a direct debit the business must complete a direct debit mandate.

This instructs its bank to pay the amounts the receiver asks for, on the dates the receiver requests payment.

Example: Direct debit mandate

Please fill in the whole form including 'the official use' box using a ball point pen and send the form to us at the address below in the envelope provided. Please do not send this instruction direct to your bank.

Instruction to your Bank or Building Society to pay by Direct Debit

NATIONAL WATER

National Water plc
PO Box 284
Donchurch
South Yorkshire
DN4 5PE

Originator's Identification Number

6	2	4	8	6	2

Name(s) of Account Holder(s)

FOR NATIONAL WATER PLC OFFICIAL USE ONLY
This is not part of the instruction to your Bank or Building Society
To be completed by customer
Please tick required option:

☐ Annually ☐ Half Yearly ☐ Monthly April to January

☐ 1st of the month ☐ 15th of the month

Bank/Building Society account number

Branch Sort Code

Name and full postal address of your Bank or Building Society

Instruction to your Bank or Building Society

Please pay National Water plc Direct Debits from the account detailed in this instruction subject to the safeguards assured by the Direct Debit Guarantee. I understand that this instruction may remain with National Water plc and if so, details will be passed electronically to my Bank/Building Society.

To: The Manager   Bank/Building Society

Address

Postcode

Signature(s)

Date

Reference Number (as shown on your water services bill)

2	2	3	0	1	7	4	0	1	2	0	1	6

Banks and Building Societies may not accept Direct Debit instructions from some types of account

The Direct Debit Guarantee

- The Guarantee is offered by all Banks and Building Societies take part in the Direct Debit Scheme. The efficiency and security of the Scheme is monitored and protected by your own Bank or Building Society.
- If the amounts to be paid or the payment dates change National Water plc will notify you 10 days in advance of your account being debited or as otherwise agreed.
- If an error is made by National Water plc or your Bank or Building Society, you are guaranteed a full and immediate refund from your branch of the amount paid.
- You can cancel a Direct Debit at any time by writing to your Bank or Building Society. Please also send a copy of your letter to us.

Effect of direct debit payments on the bank balance

Payment by direct debit reduces the payer's bank balance on the date the payment is made.

Activity 2: Payment methods (part 1)

Match each situation with the most appropriate payment method by selecting from the picklist.

Situation	Payment method
Making a monthly payment for telephone expenses.	▼
Paying for items bought over the internet from a supplier used infrequently by the business.	▼
Making a regular rent payment to the landlord. The amount payable is fixed for two years.	▼

Picklist

- Cash
- Cheque
- Credit card

- Direct debit
- Standing order

2.8 BACS (Bankers' Automated Clearing Services)

> **BACS (Bankers' Automated Clearing Services):** This is an electronic system to make payments directly from one bank account to another. They are mainly used for direct debits and direct credits from organisations.

Customers require a secure way of receiving funds and making payments. The use of cash is very limiting, and therefore in the UK many banks and building societies participate in the BACS scheme. This is a method of processing bulk payments through a system of direct debits and direct credits.

2.9 Direct credit

> **Direct credit:** A deposit of money by a payer directly into a payee's bank account.

A direct credit is a deposit of money by a payer directly into a payee's bank account. Direct credit payments are usually made electronically. This method may be used by businesses when they pay salaries and suppliers.

When making payments, details of each recipient's bank account and the amount to be paid are submitted to the BACS clearing centre. The payments are then taken directly from the business's bank account and paid into each recipient's bank account.

Effect of direct credit payments on the bank balance

Payment by direct credit reduces the payer's bank balance on the date the payment is made.

2.10 CHAPS (Clearing House Automated Payment System)

> **CHAPS:** An instruction by the business to its bank to move a large amount of money to the recipient's account at another bank so the money is available the same working day.

Unlike a cheque, A CHAPS funds transfer is performed instantaneously so there is no chance for the business to stop the payment, and the bank cannot refuse payment once it has been made, due to insufficient funds. CHAPS transfers are commonly used for large amounts such as transferring funds to solicitors for the purchase of property.

Effect of CHAPS payments on the bank balance

Payment by CHAPS reduces the payer's bank balance on the date the payment is made.

2.11 Faster payments

> **Faster payments:** A system that allows customers to make small and medium-sized payments online almost instantaneously.

Most large banks and building societies in the UK now allow their customers to make small and medium-sized payments via the internet using the **faster payments** system.

This system enables customers to send same-day payments from their bank account to the recipient's bank account.

The business must follow various security procedures to access its bank account online, then enter the recipient's details and authorise the payment.

Usually the payment is deducted immediately from the business's account, and is available almost immediately in the recipient's account (around two hours).

Effect of faster payments on the bank balance

A faster payment reduces the business's bank balance on the date of payment.

Activity 3: Effect payment methods have on the bank balance (part 2)

Identify the effect the different payment methods have on the bank balance.

Payment method	Reduce funds on the date of payment ✓	No effect ✓
Standing order		
Direct debit		
Cash withdrawal from the till		
Faster payment		

Activity 4: Payment methods (part 2)

Match each situation with the most appropriate payment method by selecting from the picklist.

Situation	Payment method
Paying the monthly payroll to employees.	▼
Paying for goods required urgently. The goods are of relatively low value; however, the supplier requires immediate payment before they are despatched.	▼
Making a payment to acquire new business premises. The funds must be transferred to the seller the same working day.	▼

Picklist

- BACS direct credit
- CHAPS
- Direct debit
- Faster payment
- Standing order

Chapter summary

- There are many ways in which businesses can make payments to suppliers and employees. The method they choose will depend on the nature of the transaction and whether or not an immediate payment is required.
- Payment methods which reduce the bank balance on the date of payment:
  - Cash withdrawn from the bank account
  - Debit card
  - Bank draft
  - Standing order
  - Direct debit
  - BACS (Bankers' Automated Clearing Services)
  - Direct credit
  - CHAPS (Clearing House Automated Payment System)
  - Faster payments.
- Payment methods which reduce the bank balance at a later date:
  - Cheque
  - Credit card.
- Payment methods which have no effect on the bank balance:
  - Cash withdrawn from the till.

Activity answers

Activity 1: Effect payment methods have on the bank balance (part 1)

The correct answers are:

Payment method	Reduce funds on the date of payment ✓	Reduce funds at a later date ✓
Cash withdrawal from bank account	✓	
Cheque		✓
Debit card	✓	
Credit card		✓

Activity 2: Payment methods (part 1)

Situation	Payment method
Making a monthly payment for telephone expenses.	Direct debit
Paying for items bought over the internet from a supplier used infrequently by the business.	Credit card
Making a regular rent payment to the landlord. The amount payable is fixed for two years.	Standing order

Activity 3: Effect payment methods have on the bank balance (part 2)

The correct answers are:

Payment method	Reduce funds on the date of payment ✓	No effect ✓
Standing order	✓	
Direct debit	✓	
Cash withdrawal from the till		✓
Faster payment	✓	

Activity 4: Payment methods (part 2)

Situation	Payment method
Paying the monthly payroll to employees.	BACS direct credit
Paying for goods required urgently. The goods are of relatively low value; however, the supplier requires immediate payment before they are despatched.	Faster payment
Making a payment to acquire new business premises. The funds must be transferred to the seller the same working day.	CHAPS

Test your learning

1 Identify whether each of the statements below is true or false.

	True ✓	False ✓
A bank draft cannot be cancelled once it has been issued.		
Any customer who pays with a debit card is taking out a loan with their bank as a result.		

2 Complete the following statements by selecting from the picklist below.

Statement	Impact on bank account
When a payment is made using a debit card, the money leaves the bank account	▼
When a payment is made using a credit card, the money leaves the bank account	▼

Picklist

- At a later date
- Immediately

3 Complete the following statements by selecting from the picklist below.

Statement	Impact on bank account
When a payment is made using BACS direct credit, the money leaves the bank account	▼
When a payment is made using CHAPS, the money leaves the bank account	▼

Picklist

- At a later date
- Immediately

4 Complete the following statements by selecting from the picklist below.

Statement	Term
In respect of cheques, the person to whom the cheque is payable is the	▼
In respect of cheques, the person writing and signing the cheque in order to make the payment is the	▼
In respect of cheques, the bank which has issued the cheque and will have to pay the cheque (ie the customer's bank) is the	▼

Picklist

- Drawee
- Drawer

- Payee

5 Complete the following sentence.

A [▼] is a method of making the same regular payment for a fixed amount directly

from a business's bank account to the bank account of a supplier.

Picklist

- Direct debit
- Standing order

 BPP

2 Bank reconciliations

Learning outcomes

2	Reconcile a bank statement with the cash book
2.2	**Use the bank statement to update the cash book**
2.2.1	Learners need to understand: reasons for reconciling the bank statement with the cash book

2.2.2	the items that can cause differences between bank statements and the cash book:
	• opening balance
	• bank interest paid/received
	• bank charges
	• automated payments/receipts
	• timing differences
	   - outstanding lodgements
	   - unpresented cheques.

2.2.3	Learners need to be able to: update the cash book using the bank statement: • unrecorded • duplicated
2.2.4	total and balance the cash book: • credit/debit balance carried down • credit/debit balance brought down.
2.3	**Complete bank reconciliation statements**

2.3.1	Learners need to be able to:
	complete bank reconciliation statements using:
	• closing bank statement balance
	• timing differences:
	   - unpresented cheques
	   - outstanding lodgements.
	• closing cash book balance.

Assessment context

There are likely to be two tasks on this topic. You will be asked to update the cash book and to complete a bank reconciliation statement. There will also be narrative questions which test your understanding of bank reconciliations.

Qualification context

Bank reconciliations are also examined in the *Financial Accounting: Preparing Financial Statements* unit.

Business context

All businesses have bank accounts which must be reconciled with the cash book so the company owners know exactly how much cash the business has at a particular point in time (eg the month end).

Chapter overview

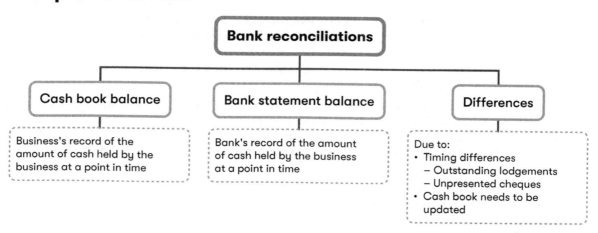

Bank reconciliations

Cash book balance

Business's record of the amount of cash held by the business at a point in time

Bank statement balance

Bank's record of the amount of cash held by the business at a point in time

Differences

Due to:
- Timing differences
  - Outstanding lodgements
  - Unpresented cheques
- Cash book needs to be updated

Introduction

Bank reconciliation statement: A statement reconciling the bank statement balance on a given date to the correct, adjusted cash book balance on the same date.

This chapter is designed to enable you to reconcile the **bank statement** with the cash book and prepare a **bank reconciliation statement**.

The cash book is used to record the detailed transactions of receipts and payments into and out of the bank account. Cash is a very important asset for the business and the company directors must be able to see how much money the company has. As a security measure, they will want to agree the balance shown in the accounting records (prepared by the accountant) to the bank statement.

Bank statements provide an independent record of the balance on the bank account **but** this balance is unlikely to agree exactly to the cash book balance – therefore a reconciliation is required.

1 Manual and digital accounting systems

In a traditional manual accounting system, on a regular basis (daily for medium and large organisations), the bookkeeper records all cash receipts and cash payments in a physical cash book. Historically, the bank would send the business a bank statement at the end of each month. The bookkeeper then reconciles items listed on the bank statement with the cash book. Any differences are investigated and resolved.

In a digital accounting system, the underlying process is similar. The cash book must be updated frequently and reconciled to the bank statement on a regular basis.

Modern banking has resulted in efficiencies in the bank reconciliation process. For example, due to electronic banking, businesses now have constant and immediate access to the bank statement. This means that reconciliations can take place more frequently, if appropriate, and any unusual items can be investigated immediately.

Sophisticated computerised accounting systems can also import the transactions listed on the business's bank statement into the accounting module.

Assessment focus point

The *Principles of Bookkeeping Controls* qualification specification document states that learners 'need to be able to update the cash book using the bank statement, and also how to complete bank reconciliation statements'.

(AAT Certificate in Accounting, Level 2, pages 44 to 45)

Therefore, the assessment will assume that the cash book and bank statement are separate reports and must be reconciled accordingly. The illustrations and activities shown in this chapter are written on this assumption.

2 Differences between the cash book balance and the bank statement

Timing differences: The reasons why the bank statement balance rarely agrees with the balance on the cash book, as receipts and payments recorded in the cash book appear later on the bank statement due to, for example, how the clearing system operates.

Outstanding lodgements: Cheques that have been received and recorded on the debit side of the cash book but do not yet appear on the bank statement.

> **Unpresented cheques:** Cheque payments that have been recorded in the credit side of the cash book but do not yet appear on the bank statement.

Differences between the cash book balance and the bank statement occur for two main reasons:

(a) **Timing differences**

When a business receives a cheque from a customer or sends a cheque to a supplier, it will update the cash book. This means the cash book balance includes this receipt or payment.

However, cheques will clear and appear on the bank statement at a later date, which results in a temporary difference in the balance per the cash book and the balance on the bank statement.

The main timing differences are:

- **Outstanding lodgements** (for example, money paid into the bank by the business but not yet appearing as a receipt on the bank statement)
- **Unpresented cheques** (for example, cheques paid out by the business which have not yet appeared on the bank statement).

(b) **The cash book has not yet been updated to include items that already appear on the bank statements**

Typical examples include:

- Standing orders (SO)
- Direct debits (DD)
- Direct credits (for example, payments made to staff for salaries, monies received electronically from credit customers)
- Bank charges
- Interest (received or charged)

Often, when a business receives the monthly bank statement it will then update the cash book to include these items.

3 Updating the cash book and performing a bank reconciliation

When updating the cash book and performing a bank reconciliation, the steps are as follows:

(a) Compare the debit side of the cash book to the paid in amounts shown on the bank statement – for each paid in amount that agrees, tick* the item in both the cash book and the bank statement.

(b) Compare the credit side of the cash book to the paid out amounts shown on the bank statement – for each paid out amount that agrees, tick the item in both the cash book and the bank statement.

(c) Any unticked items on the bank statement are items that should have been entered into the cash book but have been omitted for some reason. Enter these into the cash book and then the adjusted balance on the cash book can be calculated as usual.

(d) Finally, any unticked items in the cash book are timing differences – outstanding lodgements (debit side) and unpresented cheques (credit side) – that are used to reconcile the bank statement closing balance to the correct, adjusted cash book closing balance.

*In the AAT assessment, there may be a highlighter function which enables you to 'tick' the items.

 Illustration 1: Bank reconciliation

We will study the procedure for carrying out a bank reconciliation by looking at the cash book and bank statement for a sole trader, Dawn Fisher.

Below is a summary of the cash book of a sole trader, Dawn Fisher, for February.

Cash book – debit side

Date 20XX	Details	Bank £
2 Feb	Balance b/f	387.90
2 Feb	G Hollings	1,368.48
7 Feb	S Dancer	368.36
14 Feb	K C Ltd	2,004.37
20 Feb	F W Painter	856.09
26 Feb	J J Hammond	648.34
28 Feb	L Minns	257.50
Total		5,891.04

Note that Dawn pays in each cheque at her bank as it is received.

Cash book – credit side

Date 20XX	Details	Cheque number	Bank £
3 Feb	Long Associates	103567	1,007.46
5 Feb	Harland Bros	103568	524.71
5 Feb	L and P Timms	103569	1,035.76
8 Feb	Peter Thomas	103570	663.45
15 Feb	Gas Supplies	103571	480.50
20 Feb	F P Travel	103572	1,233.80
24 Feb	K Riley	103573	246.58
26 Feb	Farman Ltd	103574	103.64
Total			5,295.90

Dawn has just received her bank statement for the month of February.

First National

30 High Street, Benham, DR4 8TT

To: Dawn Fisher   Account number: 40268134   28 February 20XX

Date 20XX	Details	Paid out £	Paid in £	Balance £
1 Feb	Balance b/f			387.90 C
6 Feb	Transfer		1,368.48	1,756.38 C
9 Feb	Cheque no 103568	524.71		1,231.67 C
11 Feb	Transfer		368.36	

Date 20XX	Details	Paid out £	Paid in £	Balance £
	Transfer		208.34	
	Cheque no 103567	1,107.46		700.91 C
13 Feb	Cheque no 103570	663.45		37.46 C
18 Feb	Transfer		2,004.37	
	SO – FC Property	400.00		1,641.83 C
19 Feb	Cheque no 103571	480.50		1,161.33 C
24 Feb	Transfer		856.09	
	Cheque no 103569	1,035.76		981.66 C
28 Feb	Bank interest		4.84	986.50 C
28 Feb	Balance c/f			986.50 C
D = Debit, C = Credit				

Required

Prepare the bank reconciliation.

Solution

Step 1   Compare the debit side of the cash book to the paid in amounts shown on the bank statement – for each paid in amount that agrees, tick the item in both the cash book and the bank statement.

Cash book – debit side (compare with paid in column on the bank statement)

Date 20XX	Details	Bank £	
2 Feb	Balance b/f	387.90	
2 Feb	G Hollings	1,368.48	✔
7 Feb	S Dancer	368.36	✔
14 Feb	K C Ltd	2,004.37	✔
20 Feb	F W Painter	856.09	✔
26 Feb	J J Hammond	648.34	
28 Feb	L Minns	257.50	
Total		5,891.04	

Step 2   Compare the credit side of the cash book to the paid out amounts shown on the bank statement – for each paid out amount that agrees, tick the item in both the cash book and the bank statement.

Cash book – credit side (compare with paid out column on the bank statement)

Date 20XX	Details	Cheque number	Bank £	
3 Feb	Long Associates	103567	1,007.46	
5 Feb	Harland Bros	103568	524.71	✔
5 Feb	L and P Timms	103569	1,035.76	✔
8 Feb	Peter Thomas	103570	663.45	✔
15 Feb	Gas Supplies	103571	480.50	✔
20 Feb	F P Travel	103572	1,233.80	
24 Feb	K Riley	103573	246.58	
26 Feb	Farman Ltd	103574	103.64	
Total			5,295.90	

Bank statement (compare with cash book debit and credit sides)

Date 20XX	Details	Paid out £	Paid in £	Balance £
1 Feb	Balance b/f			387.90 C
6 Feb	Transfer		1,368.48 ✔	1,756.38 C
9 Feb	Cheque no 103568	524.71 ✔		1,231.67 C
11 Feb	Transfer		368.36 ✔	
	Transfer		208.34	
	Cheque no 103567	1,107.46		700.91 C
13 Feb	Cheque no 103570	663.45 ✔		37.46 C
18 Feb	Transfer		2,004.37 ✔	
	SO – FC Property	400.00		1,641.83 C
19 Feb	Cheque no 103571	480.50 ✔		1,161.33 C
24 Feb	Transfer		856.09 ✔	
	Cheque no 103569	1,035.76 ✔		981.66 C
28 Feb	Bank interest		4.84	986.50 C
28 Feb	Balance c/f			986.50 C
D = Debit, C = Credit				

Step 3   Any unticked items on the bank statement must be entered into the cash book.

Paid in amounts

- The transfer of £208.34 on 11 February has not been recorded in the debit side of the cash book, so this must be corrected.

- On 28 February an amount of £4.84 bank interest was paid into the account by the bank – this must be entered into the debit side of the cash book.

Paid out amounts

- Cheque number 103567 has been recorded in the credit side of the cash book as £1,007.46 whereas the bank statement shows it as an amount of £1,107.46. The cash book must be adjusted by including an extra £100 in the credit side.

- The SO (standing order) of £400.00 on 18 February has not been recorded in the credit side of the cash book, so it must be corrected.

Tick the items as they are written in to tie up with the bank statement and calculate the adjusted balance on the cash book. You'll find that the debit side total is higher than the credit side total, giving a balance c/d on the credit side of £308.32.

In preparation for Step 4:

The items that remain **unticked** in the cash book are timing differences that will appear on the bank reconciliation.

For learning purposes, in the illustration below these items are marked in the cash book with an R (for 'reconciling').

Cash book – debit side

Date 20XX	Details	Bank £	
2 Feb	Balance b/f	387.90	
2 Feb	G Hollings	1,368.48	✔
7 Feb	S Dancer	368.36	✔
14 Feb	K C Ltd	2,004.37	✔
20 Feb	F W Painter	856.09	✔
26 Feb	J J Hammond	648.34	R
28 Feb	L Minns	257.50	R
11 Feb	**Transfer**	**208.34**	✔
28 Feb	**Bank interest received**	**4.84**	✔
Total		6,104.22	

Cash book – credit side

Date 20XX	Details	Cheque number	Bank £	
3 Feb	Long Associates	103567	1,007.46	✔
5 Feb	Harland Bros	103568	524.71	✔
5 Feb	L and P Timms	103569	1,035.76	✔
8 Feb	Peter Thomas	103570	663.45	✔
15 Feb	Gas Supplies	103571	480.50	✔
20 Feb	F P Travel	103572	1,233.80	R
24 Feb	K Riley	103573	246.58	R

 BPP

Date 20XX	Details	Cheque number	Bank £	
26 Feb	Farman Ltd	103574	103.64	R
11 Feb	**Correction of cheque**	**103567**	**100.00**	✓
18 Feb	**FC Property**	**SO**	**400.00**	✓
28 Feb	Balance c/d		308.32	*
Total			6,104.22	

Step 4 Finally, any unticked items in the cash book are timing differences – outstanding lodgements (debit side) and unpresented cheques (credit side) – that are used to reconcile the bank statement closing balance to the correct, adjusted cash book closing balance (*calculated above as £308.32).

Bank reconciliation statement at 28 February 20XX

Bank reconciliation statement	£
Balance per bank statement	986.50
Add outstanding lodgements (from debit side)	
J J Hammond	648.34
L Minns	257.50
Total to add	905.84
Less unpresented cheques (from credit side)	
F P Travel	1,233.80
K Riley	246.58
Farman Ltd	103.64
Total to subtract	1,584.02
Balance as per correct, adjusted cash book	308.32

The bank statement and the cash book have now been reconciled and the figure that will appear in the trial balance for the bank account is the correct, adjusted cash book balance of £308.32.

4 Opening balances on the cash book and bank statement

In the illustration you may have noted that the opening balance (balance b/f) on the cash book was the same as that on the bank statement. This is because there were no unpresented cheques or outstanding lodgements at the end of the previous period.

This will not always be the case. If there were timing differences at the end of the previous period, they would have been included on the bank reconciliation statement at that date.

In the real world, when comparing this period's bank statement and cash book, you therefore need to have the previous period's bank reconciliation statement to hand in order to tick off the last period's timing differences when they appear on the bank statement in this period.

In the exam this would be a minor element of a bank reconciliation question. You would need to:

(a) Identify whether the opening balance (balance b/f) on the cash book is different to that of the bank statement; the difference will relate to an item that appears on the bank statement for the current period.

(b) Note this item on scrap paper. You do not need to include it in your exam solution, ie it should **not** be included in the cash book for the current period (as it would have been included in the cash book in the prior period).

Activity 1: Bank reconciliation – Bike Business

Bike Business received the following bank statement for September.

Date 20XX	Details	Paid out £	Paid in £	Balance £	
01 Sept	Balance b/f			10,879	C
06 Sept	Cheque 3456	2,960		7,919	C
12 Sept	Cheque 3457	4,900		3,019	C
13 Sept	Bank interest		60	3,079	C
13 Sept	Cheque 3449	1,300		1,779	C
18 Sept	Direct Debit – Elec Ltd	650		1,129	C
19 Sept	Cheque 3458	1,000		129	C
21 Sept	Transfer – PWG Ltd		6,850	6,979	C
25 Sept	Bank charges	50		6,929	C
25 Sept	Direct Debit – FRD Ltd	297		6,632	C
29 Sept	Transfer – ESD Ltd		450	7,082	C
30 Sept	Cheque 3459	2,700		4,382	C
D = Debit, C = Credit					

The cash book as at 30 September is shown after the requirements.

Required

(1) Check the items on the bank statement against the items in the cash book.

(2) Enter any items into the cash book as needed.

(3) Total the cash book and clearly show the balance carried down at 30 September AND brought down at 1 October.

(4) Identify the TWO transactions that are included in the cash book but missing from the bank statement and complete the bank reconciliation statement below as at 30 September.

Cash book

Date 20XX	Details	Bank £	Date 20XX	Cheque number	Details	Bank £
01 Sept	Balance b/f	9,579	02 Sept	3456	QSH Ltd	2,960
21 Sept	PWG Ltd	6,850	08 Sept	3457	TGM Ltd	4,900
29 Sept	WTY Ltd	590	15 Sept	3458	FTJ Ltd	1,000

Date	Details		Bank	Date	Cheque number	Details		Bank
20XX			**£**	**20XX**				**£**
	(1)	▼		18 Sept	DD	Elec Ltd		650
	(1)	▼		24 Sept	3459	YHL Ltd		2,700
	(1)	▼		30 Sept	3460	WMB Ltd		760
	(1)	▼				(1)	▼	
	(1)	▼		(1)	▼	(1)	▼	
	(1)	▼				(1)	▼	
	(1)	▼				(1)	▼	

Picklist 1

- Balance b/d
- Balance c/d
- Bank charges
- Bank interest
- Direct debit
- ESD Ltd
- FRD Ltd
- Standing order

Bank reconciliation statement	£
Balance per bank statement	
Add:	
(2) ▼	
Total to add	
Less:	
(2) ▼	
Total to subtract	
Balance as per cash book	

Picklist 2

- FRD Ltd
- FTJ Ltd
- PWG Ltd
- WMB Ltd
- WTY Ltd

5 Assessment tasks

Having looked at an illustration and activity, we will now consider assessment style tasks.

> ### Assessment focus point
>
> In the assessment, your knowledge of reconciling the cash book and performing a bank reconciliation will be tested in two tasks. It is likely that you will be asked to:
> * Check the bank statement against the cash book and enter transactions in the cash book as needed; show the cash book balance c/d and b/d
> * Review the cash book and complete a bank reconciliation statement; check that the cash book and bank statement have been correctly reconciled.
>
> To be successful in these types of tasks you need a methodical approach. Make sure you identify the items that already appear in the cash book and bank statement. You can then focus on the remaining items.

A word of warning

Remember, as we saw in Chapter 1, the bank statement shows the balance from the bank's point of view, whereas the cash book is from the business's point of view.

Therefore, should a task state that the bank account is in credit, then this means that there is a **debit** balance in the business's records.

Conversely, should a question state that the bank account balance is overdrawn, then there is a **credit** balance in the business's records. If the bank account balance is overdrawn, the business will be using the bank's overdraft facility.

> **Overdraft:** This is where the business effectively owes the bank money – it appears as a debit balance in the bank statement and a credit balance in the cash book.

Activity 2: Updating the cash book

The bank statement for November is shown below.

Bank statement

Date 20XX	Details	Paid out £	Paid in £	Balance £	
02 Nov	Balance b/f			7,890	C
05 Nov	Cheque 7823	980		6,910	C
07 Nov	Cheque 7824	4,654		2,256	C
10 Nov	Bank interest	125		2,131	C
11 Nov	Cheque 7818	230		1,901	C
18 Nov	Transfer – MPV Ltd		2,780	4,681	C
20 Nov	Cheque 7825	650		4,031	C
24 Nov	Standing order – A Motor Co	500		3,531	C
25 Nov	Cheque 7826	410		3,121	C
25 Nov	Direct debit – SAO Ltd	730		2,391	C

Date	Details		Paid out	Paid in	Balance	
20XX			£	£	£	
28 Nov	Transfer – WD Ltd			476	2,867	C
30 Nov	Bank charges		75		2,792	C
D = Debit, C = Credit						

The cash book as at 30 November is shown after the requirement.

Required

Check the bank statement against the cash book and enter:

- **Any transactions into the cash book as needed**
- **The cash book balance carried down at 30 November and brought down at 1 December**

Cash book

Date	Details	Bank	Date	Cheque number	Details	Bank
20XX		£	20XX			£
01 Nov	Balance b/f	7,660	01 Nov	7823	RFT Ltd	980
18 Nov	MPV Ltd	2,780	02 Nov	7824	JGB Ltd	4,654
28 Nov	NON Ltd	420	15 Nov	7825	DER Ltd	650
	▼		20 Nov	7826	WTR Ltd	410
	▼		25 Nov	Direct debit	SAO Ltd	730
	▼		28 Nov	7827	REW Ltd	147
	▼		30 Nov	7828	YLK Ltd	589
	▼				▼	
	▼			▼	▼	
	▼				▼	
	▼				▼	
	▼				▼	

Picklist

- A Motor Co
- Balance b/d
- Balance c/d
- Bank charges
- Bank interest
- Direct debit
- Standing order
- WD Ltd

Activity 3: Bank reconciliation statement

Below is the bank statement for June.

Bank statement

Date 20XX	Details	Paid out £	Paid in £	Balance £	
01 June	Balance b/f			385	D
07 June	Transfer – PKL Ltd		4,000	3,615	C
08 June	Cheque 007303	250		3,365	C
08 June	Cheque 007315	483		2,882	C
14 June	Cheque 007316	2,165		717	C
15 June	Cheque 007317	1,233		516	D
20 June	Direct debit Hampton CC	135		651	D
20 June	Direct debit Motor Mania	177		828	D
21 June	Transfer – Bissell & Co		2,500	1,672	C
22 June	Bank charges	44		1,628	C
22 June	Bank interest		3	1,631	C
D = Debit, C = Credit					

The cash book and bank reconciliation statement for June have not yet been finalised.

Cash book

Date 20XX	Details	Bank £	Date 20XX	Cheque number	Details	Bank £
15 June	PKL Ltd	4,000	01 June		Balance b/f	635
20 June	Beaker plc	3,245	01 June	07315	Abby Photos	483
21 June	Bissell & Co	2,500	06 June	07316	LTL Ltd	2,165
22 June	Gilchrist Ltd	2,416	06 June	07317	Retro Frames	1,233
22 June	Bank interest	3	22 June	07318	Tonks & Co	1,020
			22 June	07319	Taylor Agencies	547
			20 June	Direct debit	Hampton CC	135
			20 June	Direct debit	Motor Mania	177
			22 June		Bank charges	44

Required

(a) Identify the FOUR transactions that are included in the cash book but missing from the bank statement and complete the bank reconciliation statement below as at 22 June.

Do not enter figures with minus signs or brackets in this task. Do not make any entries in the shaded boxes.

Bank reconciliation statement		£
Balance per bank statement		
Add:		
▼		
▼		
Total to add		
Less:		
▼		
▼		
Total to subtract		
Balance as per cash book		

Picklist

- Abby Photos
- Beaker plc
- Bissell & Co
- Direct Debit
- Gilchrist Ltd
- Hampton CC
- LTL Ltd
- Motor Mania
- PKL Ltd
- Retro Frames
- Taylor Agencies
- Tonks & Co

(b) Refer to the cash book and check that the bank statement has been correctly reconciled by calculating:

- The balance carried down
- The total of each of the bank columns after the balance carried down has been recorded

Balance carried down £	Bank column totals £

6 Duplicating entries in the cash book

When the cash book and bank statement are reconciled, it may be found that the bookkeeper has accidently duplicated the posting of a transaction in the cash book.

Illustration 2: Error of duplication

This is a cash book for Osman.

Cash book – Debit side			Cash book – Credit side		
Date 20XX	Details	Bank £	Date 20XX	Details	Bank £
2 Apr	Balance b/f	1,200	12 Apr	H Torr	700
16 Apr	N Gate	380	14 Apr	L Dee	640
28 Apr	L Shar	75	26 Apr	Bank charges	60
14 Feb	F Peters	1,645	26 Apr	Bank charges	60
			30 Apr	Balance c/d	1,840
		3,300			3,300
1 May	Balance b/d	1,840			

The credit side includes a duplicated entry in relation to bank charges of £60.

Required

After correcting the duplicated entry in the cash book, what is the balance b/d in the cash book on 1 May? Show whether the balance is a debit or credit item.

£	Debit/credit entry
	▼

Picklist

- Credit
- Debit

Solution

£	Debit/credit entry
1,900	Debit

The balance b/d in the unadjusted cash book is £1,840 debit. However, the credit entry of £60 bank charges has been posted twice on the credit side of the cash book. One of the credit postings of £60 must be removed from the cash book. £60 is therefore added back to the debit balance of £1,840. Working: £1,840 + £60 = £1,900.

Chapter summary

- To ensure the accuracy of the cash book, it must be checked at regular intervals to bank statements received.

- Differences between the cash book balance and the bank statement arise due to timing differences (mainly outstanding lodgements and unpresented cheques) and also if the cash book has not yet been updated to include items that only appear on the bank statement.

- When updating the cash book and performing a bank reconciliation, the steps are as follows:

  (1) Compare the debit side of the cash book to the paid in amounts shown on the bank statement – for each paid in amount that agrees, tick the item in both the cash book and the bank statement.

  (2) Compare the credit side of the cash book to the paid out amounts shown on the bank statement – for each paid out amount that agrees, tick the item in both the cash book and the bank statement.

  (3) Any unticked items on the bank statement (other than errors made by the bank) are items that should have been entered into the cash book but have been omitted for some reason. Enter these into the cash book and then the adjusted balance on the cash book can be calculated as usual.

  (4) Finally, any unticked items in the cash book are timing differences – outstanding lodgements (debit side) and unpresented cheques (credit side) – that are used to reconcile the bank statement closing balance to the correct, adjusted cash book closing balance.

- The closing balance on the bank statement is reconciled to the correct, adjusted closing cash book balance in the bank reconciliation statement.

- Any duplicated items must be removed from the cash book and the closing balance re-calculated so that the balance c/d and b/d in the adjusted cash book is correct.

Activity answers

Activity 1: Bank reconciliation – Bike Business

Cash book

Date	Details	Bank	Date	Cheque number	Details	Bank
20XX		£	20XX			£
01 Sept	Balance b/f	9,579	02 Sept	3456	QSH Ltd	2,960
21 Sept	PWG Ltd	6,850	08 Sept	3457	TGM Ltd	4,900
29 Sept	WTY Ltd	590	15 Sept	3458	FTJ Ltd	1,000
13 Sept	Bank interest	60	18 Sept	DD	Elec Ltd	650
29 Sept	ESD Ltd	450	24 Sept	3459	YHL Ltd	2,700
			30 Sept	3460	WMB Ltd	760
			25 Sept		Bank charges	50
			25 Sept	Direct debit	FRD Ltd	297
			30 Sept		Balance c/d	4,212
		17,529				17,529
1 Oct	Balance b/d	4,212				

Bank reconciliation statement	£
Balance per bank statement	4,382
Add:	
WTY Ltd	590
Total to add	590
Less:	
WMB Ltd	760
Total to subtract	760
Balance as per cash book	4,212

Difference in opening balances

The balance b/f on the bank statement at 1 September is £10,879.

The balance b/f on the cash book is £9,579.

Difference of £1,300 (due to cheque 3449 which would have been included in last month's bank reconciliation statement).

Having compared the cash book with the bank statement and ticked the items that are already included in both documents, we can see there are several items that need to be added to the cash book or included on the bank reconciliation statement.

Cash book

 BPP

The paid-in side of the bank statement shows bank interest of £60 and a receipt from ESD Ltd of £450. These items are not yet included in the cash book and therefore must be recorded on the debit side, as they are an increase to the cash book balance.

Similarly, the paid-out side of the bank statement shows bank charges of £50 and a direct debit payment to FRD Ltd of £297. These items are not yet included in the cash book and therefore must be recorded on the credit side, as they are a decrease to the cash book balance.

Bank statement

The receipt from WTY Ltd of £590 is on the debit side of the cash book. When it clears, the bank statement it will increase the balance. Therefore, it is included under the Add heading.

The payment to WMB Ltd of £760 is on the credit side of the cash book. Therefore, when it clears, the bank statement it will decrease the bank balance. For this reason, it is included under the Less heading.

Activity 2: Updating the cash book

Cash book

Date	Details	Bank	Date	Cheque number	Details	Bank
20XX		£	20XX			£
01 Nov	Balance b/f	7,660	01 Nov	7823	RFT Ltd	980
18 Nov	MPV Ltd	2,780	02 Nov	7824	JGB Ltd	4,654
28 Nov	NON Ltd	420	15 Nov	7825	DER Ltd	650
28 Nov	**WD Ltd**	**476**	20 Nov	7826	WTR Ltd	410
			25 Nov	Direct debit	SAO Ltd	730
			28 Nov	7827	REW Ltd	147
			30 Nov	7828	YLK Ltd	589
			10 Nov		**Bank interest**	125
			24 Nov	Standing order	A Motor Co	500
			30 Nov		Bank charges	75
			30 Nov		Balance c/d	2,476
		11,336				11,336
1 Dec	Balance b/d	2,476				

Difference in opening balances

The balance b/f 2 November on the bank statement is £7,890.

The balance b/f in the cash book is £7,660.

Difference of £230 (due to cheque 7818 which would have been included in last month's bank reconciliation statement).

Cash book

The paid-in side of the bank statement includes a receipt from WD Ltd of £476. This item is not yet included in the cash book and therefore must be recorded on the debit side, as it increases the cash book balance.

The paid-out side of the bank statement contains several items that reduce the bank balance and need to be entered on the credit side of the cash book. The items are bank interest (£125), A Motor Co (£500) and bank charges (£75).

 BPP

Activity 3: Bank reconciliation statement

(a)

Bank reconciliation statement	£
Balance per bank statement	1,631
Add:	
Beaker plc	3,245
Gilchrist Ltd	2,416
Total to add	5,661
Less:	
Tonks & Co	1,020
Taylor Agencies	547
Total to subtract	1,567
Balance as per cash book	5,725

Difference in opening balances

The balance b/f in the cash book is £635.

The balance b/f on the bank statement is £385.

Difference of £250 (due to cheque 007303 which would have been included in last month's bank reconciliation statement).

Bank reconciliation

Having compared the cash book with the bank statement and ticked the items that are included in both documents, we can see that there are four items in the cash book that are missing from the bank statement.

The receipts from Beaker plc of £3,245 and Gilchrist Ltd of £2,416 are on the debit side of the cash book but not shown on the bank statement. This means that when they clear, the bank statement will show an increase in the bank balance. Therefore, they are included under the Add heading of the reconciliation statement.

The payments to Tonks & Co of £1,020 and Taylor Agencies of £547 are on the credit side of the cash book. Therefore, when they clear, the bank statement will show a decrease in the bank balance. For this reason, they are included under the Less heading.

(b)

Balance carried down	Bank column totals
£	£
5,725	12,164

The debit side of the cash book is the higher of the two sides, and gives a bank column total of £12,164. When adding up the transactions on the credit side of the cash book, the amount is initially £6,439. By inserting a balance carried down of £5,725 (£12,164 minus £6,439), the debit side bank column total equals the credit side bank total column, and the cash book balances.

This also proves the reconciliation is correct as the balance c/d per the cash book is the same as the balance calculated through the reconciliation statement.

BPP

Cash book

Date	Details	Bank	Date	Cheque number	Details	Bank
20XX		£	20XX			£
15 June	PKL Ltd	4,000	01 June		Balance b/f	635
20 June	Beaker plc	3,245	01 June	07315	Abby Photos	483
21 June	Bissell & Co	2,500	06 June	07316	LTL Ltd	2,165
22 June	Gilchrist Ltd	2,416	06 June	07317	Retro Frames	1,233
22 June	Bank interest	3	22 June	07318	Tonks & Co	1,020
			22 June	07319	Taylor Agencies	547
			20 June	Direct debit	Hampton CC	135
			20 June	Direct debit	Motor Mania	177
			22 June		Bank charges	44
			22 June		**Balance c/d**	**5,725**
		12,164				**12,164**

 BPP

Test your learning

1 If money is paid into a newly opened bank current account this will appear on the bank statement as (tick the appropriate option):

	✓
A debit entry	
A credit entry	

2 If a figure for bank interest appeared in the paid in column of the bank statement, this would be adjusted for in the (tick the appropriate option):

	✓
Debit side of the cash book	
Credit side of the cash book	

3 A standing order payment is on the bank statement but has been omitted from the cash book. This should be adjusted for in the (tick the appropriate option):

	✓
Debit side of the cash book	
Credit side of the cash book	

4 A cheque in the credit side of the cash book is unticked after the bank statement and cash book have been compared.

Required

How should this be dealt with in the bank reconciliation statement? (Tick the appropriate option):

	✓
As an unpresented cheque	
As an outstanding lodgement	

5 Bremner Ltd received the following bank statement for February.

Date	Details	Paid out	Paid in	Balance	
20XX		£	£	£	
03 Feb	Balance b/f			6,230	C
03 Feb	Cheque 003252	2,567		3,663	C
03 Feb	Cheque 003253	333		3,330	C
03 Feb	Cheque 003254	1,006		2,324	C
04 Feb	Cheque 003257	3,775		1,451	D

Date	Details		Paid out	Paid in	Balance	
20XX			£	£	£	
09 Feb	Branthill Co			1,559	108	C
11 Feb	Cheque 003255		966		858	D
13 Feb	Direct debit – AxDC		250		1,108	D
18 Feb	Direct debit – Trust Insurance		325		1,433	D
20 Feb	Bank charges		14		1,447	D
22 Feb	Interest charge		56		1,503	D
23 Feb	Transfer			2,228	725	C
D = Debit, C = Credit						

The cash book as at 23 February is shown after the requirements.

Required

(1) Check the items on the bank statement against the items in the cash book.

(2) Using the picklist below for the details column, enter any items in the cash book as needed.

(3) Total the cash book and clearly show the balance carried down at 23 February and brought down at 24 February.

(4) Identify the four transactions that are included in the cash book but missing from the bank statement, and complete the bank reconciliation statement as at 23 February using the picklist.

Cash book

Date	Details	Bank	Date	Cheque number	Details	Bank
20XX		£	**20XX**			£
01 Feb	Balance b/f	6,230	01 Feb	003252	Jeggers Ltd	2,567
20 Feb	Straightens Co	2,228	01 Feb	003253	Short & Fell	333
21 Feb	Plumpers	925	01 Feb	003254	Rastop Ltd	1,006
22 Feb	Eastern Supplies	1,743	01 Feb	003255	A & D Trading	966
	▼		02 Feb	003256	Jesmond Warr	2,309
	▼		02 Feb	003257	Nistral Ltd	3,775
	▼		13 Feb	003258	Simpsons	449
	▼		13 Feb		AxDC	250
	▼				▼	
	▼				▼	
	▼				▼	
	▼				▼	

Date	Details		Bank	Date	Cheque number	Details		Bank
20XX			£	20XX				£
		▼					▼	

Bank reconciliation statement as at 23 February 20XX

Bank reconciliation statement		£
Balance per bank statement		
Add:		
	▼	
	▼	
Total to add		
Less:		
	▼	
	▼	
Total to subtract		
Balance as per cash book		

Picklist

- A & D Trading
- AxDC
- Balance b/d
- Balance c/d
- Bank charges
- Branthill Co
- Closing balance
- DD Trust Insurance
- Eastern Supplies
- Interest charge
- Jeggers Ltd
- Jesmond Warr
- Nistral Ltd
- Opening balance
- Pumpers
- Rastop Ltd
- Short & Fell
- Simpsons
- Straightens Co

3 Introduction to control accounts

Learning outcomes

1	**Use control accounts**
1.1	**Produce control accounts**
1.1.1	Learners need to understand:
	the purpose of the receivables and payables ledger control accounts (part of the double entry bookkeeping system)
1.1.2	the purpose of the VAT control account.
1.1.3	Learners need to be able to:
	prepare control accounts:
	• receivables ledger
	• payables ledger
	• VAT
1.1.4	total and balance control accounts:
	• balance carried down
	• balance brought down.
1.2	**Reconcile control accounts**
1.2.1	Learners need to understand:
	reasons for reconciling the receivables and payables ledger control accounts with the receivables and payables ledgers.
1.2.2	Learners need to be able to:
	total the balances of the individual receivables and payables ledger accounts:
	• receivables ledger debit/credit balances
	• payables ledger debit/credit balances
1.2.3	identify discrepancies between the receivables and payables ledger control accounts and the individual customer and supplier accounts
1.2.4	identify reasons for discrepancies between the receivables and payables ledger control accounts and the individual customer and supplier accounts.

Assessment context

Control accounts are a key part of the syllabus. You need to understand the purpose of the receivables, payables VAT control account and the reasons why the receivables ledger control account is reconciled with the receivables ledger, and the payables ledger control account reconciled with the payables ledger. This sets the scene for the questions we will see in the next chapter and could be tested in a knowledge-based task. The VAT control account is another general ledger account and one which you should learn how to prepare.

Qualification context

In the *Financial Accounting: Preparing Financial Statements* unit you could be required to identify the reasons why reconciliations are carried out, as well as to determine the adjustments that may need to be made to the control account balance and/or the individual receivables or payables ledger balance.

Business context

Businesses must be able to account for their customers and suppliers efficiently and accurately. This enables them to chase up overdue balances from credit customers and ensure that their suppliers are paid on a timely basis. They must also identify VAT transactions and make appropriate payments to HMRC.

Chapter overview

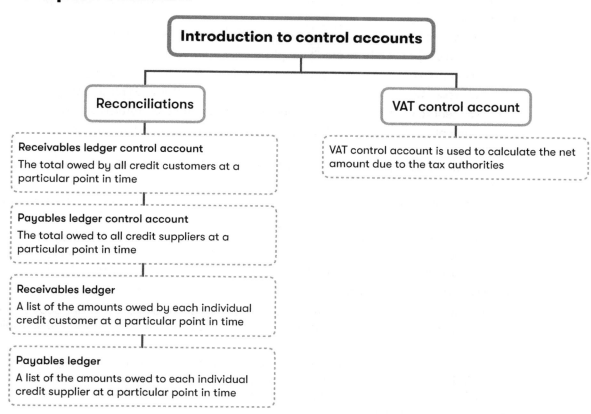

Introduction to control accounts

Reconciliations

Receivables ledger control account

The total owed by all credit customers at a particular point in time

Payables ledger control account

The total owed to all credit suppliers at a particular point in time

Receivables ledger

A list of the amounts owed by each individual credit customer at a particular point in time

Payables ledger

A list of the amounts owed to each individual credit supplier at a particular point in time

VAT control account

VAT control account is used to calculate the net amount due to the tax authorities

Introduction

In earlier studies we have seen that business transactions are recorded in the books of prime entry. In particular:

(a) Sales invoices sent to credit customers are recorded in the sales day book

(b) Purchase invoices received from credit suppliers are recorded in the purchases day book

(c) Cash received from customers or paid to suppliers is noted in the cash book

(d) Credit notes received from credit customers are recorded in the sales returns day book

(e) Credit notes sent to credit suppliers are recorded in the purchases returns day book

(f) Prompt payments discounts taken by credit customers are recorded in the discounts allowed day book

(g) Prompt payments discounts given by credit suppliers are recorded in the discounts received day book.

Having been recorded in the day books, these transactions will then be included in the relevant ledgers.

As was seen in the *Introduction to Bookkeeping* course book, the mechanism for including transactions in the relevant ledger varies according to whether a manual accounting system or a digital accounting system is used. However, the same process is followed in both situations.

Posting from the books of prime entry to the ledgers in a manual system

If a manual system is used then once a transaction has been entered in the relevant book of prime entry, the bookkeeper will need to separately post it to both the general ledger and the subsidiary ledgers.

In the case of posting transactions to the general ledger, as we have seen periodically the day books are totalled and the **totals** are posted to the general ledger. However, in respect of the subsidiary receivables and payables ledgers, transactions are posted individually to the receivables and payables ledgers.

Posting from the books of prime entry to the ledgers in digital system

If a digital system is used, once a transaction has been entered in the relevant book of prime entry it will automatically be posted to the general ledger. If the transaction relates to a credit sale or purchase, it will also automatically be posted to the relevant receivables or payables ledger. This is more efficient than making separate postings. It also reduces the risks of errors occurring as there are fewer manual entries. It is, therefore, one of the benefits of a digital system.

In a digital accounting system, as the general ledger and the associated receivables or payables ledgers are updated automatically from the same source, the total of the receivables ledger control account will always equal the total of the subsidiary receivables ledger accounts. Likewise, the total of the payables ledger control account will always equal the total of the subsidiary payables ledger accounts.

Manual system

For the purposes of the assessment, this chapter will focus on reconciling discrepancies which arise in a manual accounting system.

In this situation all day books are totalled periodically and the totals are posted to the relevant **control account** (which forms part of the double entry bookkeeping system). Individual items are posted to the ledger accounts (which sit outside the main ledger).

Three important control accounts are:

(a) **Receivables ledger control account** – which shows the amount owed by credit customers

(b) **Payables ledger control account** – which shows the amount owed to credit suppliers

(c) **VAT control account** – which shows the amount due or reclaimable from HMRC.

The receivables ledger control account is supported by the **receivables ledger** and the payables ledger control account is supported by the **payables ledger**.

1 Recap from earlier studies

1.1 Recording credit sales and purchases in the general ledger (recap)

From your previous accounting studies you are familiar with the concept that credit sales and purchases (and any returns that arise) are entered in the main ledger with the following journals:

(a) **Main ledger – total credit sales for a particular period**

Account name	Debit	Credit
	✔	✔
Receivables ledger control	✔	
VAT		✔
Sales		✔

(b) **Main ledger – total credit sales returns for a particular period**

Account name	Debit	Credit
	✔	✔
Sales returns	✔	
VAT	✔	
Receivables ledger control		✔

(c) **Main ledger – total purchases for a particular period**

Account name	Debit	Credit
	✔	✔
Purchases	✔	
VAT	✔	
Payables ledger control		✔

(d) **Main ledger – total purchases returns for a particular period**

Account name	Debit	Credit
	✔	✔
Payables ledger control	✔	
VAT		✔
Purchases returns		✔

Activity 1: Double entry (credit sales)

In the month of January, a VAT-registered business makes sales on credit of £20,000 excluding VAT.

Required

What is the double entry to record this in the general ledger?

Account name		Amount £	Debit ✓	Credit ✓
▼				
▼				
▼				

Picklist

- Bank
- Payables ledger control
- Purchases
- Purchases returns
- Receivables ledger control
- Sales
- Sales returns
- VAT

Activity 2: Double entry (credit purchases)

In the month of January, a VAT-registered business makes purchases on credit of £10,000 excluding VAT.

Required

What is the double entry to record this in the general ledger?

Account name		Amount £	Debit ✓	Credit ✓
▼				
▼				
▼				

Picklist

- Bank
- Payables ledger control
- Purchases
- Purchases returns
- Receivables ledger control
- Sales
- Sales returns
- VAT

1.2 Prompt payment discounts (recap)

When a credit customer takes advantage of a prompt payment discount, this must be recorded in the ledgers. The entries are as follows.

Discounts allowed

Main ledger – discounts allowed

Account name	Debit	Credit
	✓	✓
Discounts allowed	✓	
VAT	✓	
Receivables ledger control		✓

The credit entry to the receivables ledger control account balance is for the gross amount as the full amount settled by way of the discount is no longer owed by the customer. The VAT element is posted to the VAT account, cancelling out the VAT which arose on the original sale. The net amount is posted as a debit to the discounts allowed account, being an increase in expenses.

Receivables ledger – discounts allowed

Account name	Debit	Credit
	✓	✓
Customer X		✓

The receivables ledger is credited with the full amount (gross amount) settled by way of the discount as this is no longer owed by the customer.

Discounts received

Main ledger – discounts received

Account name	Debit	Credit
	✓	✓
Payables ledger control	✓	
VAT		✓
Discounts received		✓

The debit entry to the payables ledger control account is for the gross amount as the full amount settled by way of the discount is no longer owed to the supplier. The VAT element is posted to the VAT account, cancelling out the VAT which arose on the original purchase. The net amount is posted as a credit to the discounts received account, being an increase in income.

Payables ledger – discounts received

Account name	Debit	Credit
	✓	✓
Supplier Y	✓	

The payables ledger is debited with the full amount settled by way of the discount as this is no longer owed to the supplier.

2 Control accounts

2.1 Purpose of control accounts

Control account: A general ledger account that includes totals from the books of prime entry. This helps ensure that postings to the general ledger are complete and accurate.

Control accounts contain summarised totals of all the individual transactions affecting their respective ledgers. They contain the same information as is in the receivables and payables accounts in the ledgers; however, they show the totals rather than the individual transactions.

Control accounts are mainly used for trade receivables (credit customers), trade payables (credit suppliers) and VAT.

The receivables ledger control account is an account in which records are kept of transactions involving all credit customers in total.

A payables ledger control account is an account in which records are kept of transactions involving all credit suppliers in total.

The control account system therefore means the following:

(a) Transactions posted to the general ledger are kept to a minimum so there is less room for error in the general ledger double entry system.

(b) It is easy at any point in time to identify from the general ledger how much in total the business owes and is owed.

(c) The accuracy of the general ledger and the **subsidiary ledgers** can be checked by reconciling the balance on the control account in the former to the total of the balances on the latter. This prompts the business to identify and deal with discrepancies quickly.

(d) Segregation of duties is promoted within the organisation as one person could maintain the receivables and payables ledger accounts and another person could maintain the control accounts. This reduces the risk of fraud.

Also, and as you have seen when preparing an initial trial balance in earlier studies, control accounts are general ledger accounts which form part of the double entry bookkeeping system. Therefore the year-end balances are ultimately included in the final accounts.

2.2 Preparing control accounts

Receivables ledger control account: Totals for all the credit sales transactions are posted to this account.

Payables ledger control account: Totals for all the credit purchases transactions are posted to this account.

A typical receivables ledger control account will be structured as follows:

Receivables ledger control

Details	Amount £	Details	Amount £
Balance b/d	X	Bank	X
Credit sales	X	Sales returns	X
		Discounts allowed	X
		Balance c/d	X
	X		X
Balance b/d	X		

Explanation

Details	Explanation
Balance b/d	This is normally on the left-hand side of the receivables ledger control account. This is because the credit customers owe money to the business and therefore the balance b/d is an asset.
Balance c/d	This is a balancing figure which enables the totals on both sides of the T-account to equal each other. It is usually a balancing figure on the right-hand side of the T-account.
Credit sales	Credit sales increase the amount owed by credit customers. Therefore a debit entry is posted to the control account, reflecting the increase in the asset.
Bank	When credit customers pay the amount they owe there is a decrease in the receivables ledger control account asset. Therefore this entry is on the right-hand side of the account.
Sales returns	Sales returns decrease the asset as the customers have returned the items they originally bought, and therefore no longer owe money to the business. Therefore this entry is on the right-hand side of the account.
Discounts allowed	If amounts owed by credit customers are partially settled through discounts allowed, this also reduces the receivables ledger control account asset. Therefore this entry is on the right-hand side of the account.

A typical payables ledger control account will be structured as follows:

Payables ledger control

Details	Amount £	Details	Amount £
Bank	X	Balance b/d	X
Purchases returns	X	Credit purchases	X
Discounts received	X		
Balance c/d	X		
	X		X
		Balance b/d	X

Explanation

Details	Explanation
Balance b/d	This is normally on the right-hand side of the payables ledger control account. This is because the business owes money to the credit supplier and therefore the balance b/d is a liability.
Balance c/d	This is a balancing figure which enables the totals on both sides of the T-account to equal each other. It is usually a balancing figure on the left-hand side of the T-account.
Credit purchases	Credit purchases increase the liability as the business owes suppliers for the items bought on credit. Therefore this entry is to the credit side of the account.

Details	Explanation
Bank	When credit suppliers are paid the amount owed there is a decrease in the payables ledger control account liability. Therefore this entry is on the left-hand side of the account.
Purchases returns	Purchases returns decrease the liability as the business has returned the items it originally bought, and therefore no longer owes money to the supplier. Therefore this entry is on the left-hand side of the account.
Discount received	If an amount owed to credit suppliers is partially settled through a discount, this reduces the payables ledger control account liability. Therefore this entry is also on the left-hand side of the account.

3 Purpose of subsidiary ledger accounts

Subsidiary ledgers: The receivables ledger and payables ledger, which contain a ledger account for each individual credit customer or credit supplier. They are not part of the general ledger.

Receivables ledger: Contains separate accounts for each credit customer so that, at any time, a business knows how much it is owed by each customer.

Payables ledger: Contains separate accounts for each credit supplier so that, at any time, a business knows how much it owes to each supplier.

Subsidiary ledger accounts are prepared so that the business can see the amount owed from credit customers or to credit suppliers at a point in time. The receivables ledger contains separate accounts for each credit customer and the payables ledger contains separate accounts for each credit supplier. The separate accounts list all transactions (invoices, credit notes, payments etc) relating to individual credit customers/suppliers.

If the double entry in the general ledger and the entries in the subsidiary ledger have all been entered correctly, the total of the list of balances in the ledgers will always equal the balance on the respective control account.

Illustration 1: The accounting system for credit sales

We will see how the receivables ledger and receivables ledger control accounts are created and reconciled through an illustration.

W Johnson has two credit customers, A and B. On 1 May 20XX, Customer A owes £300 and Customer B owes £170 (therefore £470 in total).

In May the following transactions occur and are recorded in the day books.

The sales day book is used to record all invoices sent to customers buying on credit.

Sales day book (extract)

Date	Details	Invoice number	Total	VAT	Net
20XX			£	£	£
3 May	A	0045	240	40	200
8 May	B	0046	180	30	150
20 May	B	0047	120	20	100
28 May	A	0048	216	36	180

Date	Details	Invoice number	Total	VAT	Net
20XX			£	£	£
	Totals		756	126	630

If items are returned by customers, credit notes are recorded in the sales returns day book.

Sales returns day book (extract)

Date 20XX	Details	Credit note number	Total	VAT	Net
20XX			£	£	£
12 May	A	CN012	240	40	200
30 May	B	CN015	120	20	100
	Totals		360	60	300

Money received from credit customers is entered in the debit side of the cash book

Cash book – debit side (extract)

Date	Details	Bank	Receivables ledger control
20XX		£	£
21 May	A	276	276
25 May	B	170	170
	Totals	446	446

Where the customer decides to take a prompt payment discount, the business issues a credit note which is recorded in the discounts allowed day book.

Discounts allowed day book (extract)

Details	Total	VAT	Net
	£	£	£
Customer A	24	4	20
Totals	24	4	20

Having recorded the transactions in the day books, the business then needs to understand:

- The amount owed by customers A and B at the end of the month
- The effect these transactions have on the general ledger.

Receivables ledger

The subsidiary receivables ledger for W Johnson in May will be as follows:

Customer A – Receivables ledger account

Details	Amount	Details	Amount
	£		£
Balance b/d	300	Credit note	240

Details	Amount £	Details	Amount £
Invoice	240	Bank	276
Invoice	216	Discounts allowed	24
		Balance c/d	216
	756		756
Balance b/d	216		

Customer B – Receivables ledger account

Details	Amount £	Details	Amount £
Balance b/d	170	Credit note	120
Invoice	180	Bank	170
Invoice	120	Balance c/d	180
	470		470
Balance b/d	180		

Therefore it can be seen that the receivables ledger accounts show the amount owed by each individual customer at a point in time.

Receivables ledger control account

The receivables ledger control account for W Johnson in May will be as follows:

Receivables ledger control account

Details	Amount £	Details	Amount £
Balance b/d	470	Sales returns	360
Sales	756	Bank	446
		Discounts allowed	24
		Balance c/d	396
	1,226		1,226
Balance b/d	396		

In this illustration for W Johnson, it can be seen that the closing balance b/d in the receivables ledger control account at the end of the month equals the total of the individual balances on the receivables ledgers accounts for customers A and B.

Reconciliation

Details	Amount £
Customer A	216

Details	Amount £
Customer B	180
Total of the receivables ledger account balances	396
Balance b/d at the end of May in the receivables ledger control account	396
Difference	nil

This suggests that the transactions have been correctly recorded in the accounting records.

4 Diagram – accounting system for credit sales

This whole process of accounting for credit sales in the general ledger and in the receivables ledger, ignoring credit notes and discounts for now, can be illustrated in a diagram:

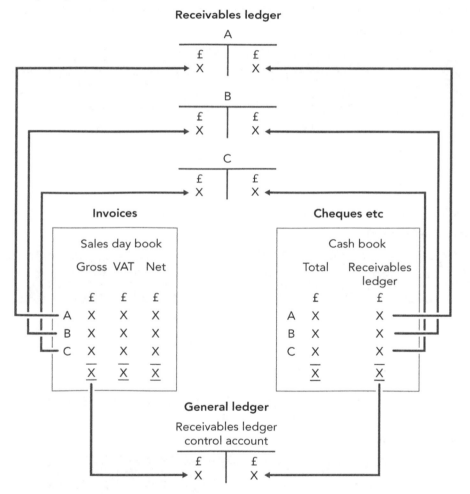

 Illustration 2: The accounting system for credit purchases

In this next illustration we will see how the subsidiary payables ledger and payables ledger control account are created and reconciled.

W Johnson purchases goods on credit from suppliers C and D. On 1 May 20XX W Johnson owes supplier C £250 and owes supplier D £140 (therefore £390 in total).

In May, the following transactions occur and are recorded in the day books.

The purchases day book is used to record all invoices received from suppliers when purchasing on credit.

Purchases day book (extract)

Date 20XX	Details	Invoice number	Total	VAT	Net
			£	£	£
5 May	C	CC10	96	16	80
10 May	C	CC18	144	24	120
15 May	D	LV73	90	15	75
27 May	D	LV80	252	42	210
	Totals		582	97	485

If items are returned to suppliers, credit notes are recorded in the purchases returns day book.

Purchases returns day book (extract)

Date 20XX	Details	Credit note number	Total	VAT	Net
			£	£	£
12 May	C	CN33	96	16	80
30 May	D	CN104	252	42	210
	Totals		348	58	290

Money paid to credit suppliers is entered in the credit side of the cash book.

Cash book – credit side (extract)

Date 20XX	Details	Bank	Payables ledger control
		£	£
21 May	C	250	250
25 May	D	128	128
34	Totals	378	378

Where the business decides to take a prompt payment discount, the credit note detailing this transaction is recorded in the discounts received day book.

Discounts received day book (extract)

Details	Total	VAT	Net
	£	£	£
Supplier D	12	2	10
Totals	12	2	10

Payables ledger

The subsidiary payables ledger for W Johnson in May will be as follows:

Supplier C – Payables ledger account

Details	Amount £	Details	Amount £
Credit note	96	Balance b/d	250
Bank	250	Invoice	96
Balance c/d	144	Invoice	144
	490		490
		Balance b/d	144

Supplier D – Payables ledger account

Details	Amount £	Details	Amount £
Credit note	252	Balance b/d	140
Bank	128	Invoice	90
Discount received	12	Invoice	252
Balance c/d	90		
	482		482
		Balance b/d	90

The payables ledger control account for W Johnson in May will be as follows:

Payables ledger control account

Details	Amount £	Details	Amount £
Purchases returns	348	Balance b/d	390
Bank	378	Credit purchases	582
Discounts received	12		
Balance c/d	234		
	972		972
		Balance b/d	234

In this illustration for W Johnson, it can be seen that the closing balance b/d in the payables ledger control account at the end of the month equals the total of the individual balances on the payables ledger accounts for suppliers C and D.

Reconciliation

Details	Amount £
Supplier C	144

Details	Amount £
Supplier D	90
Total of the subsidiary payables ledger account balances	234
Balance b/d at the end of May in the payables ledger control account	234
Difference	nil

This suggests that the transactions have been correctly recorded in the accounting records.

Regular reconciliations between the control account and ledger help to ensure that the accounting records are accurate as discrepancies can quickly be identified and corrected.

However, note that it does not prevent all errors from occurring. For example, if a purchase invoice was accidentally omitted from the purchases day book, this would not be identified by a reconciliation as both the payables ledger and payables ledger control account would be understated in respect of this transaction.

5 Diagram – accounting system for credit purchases

This whole process of accounting for credit purchases in the general ledger and in the payables ledger, ignoring credit notes and discounts, can be illustrated in a diagram:

Payables ledger

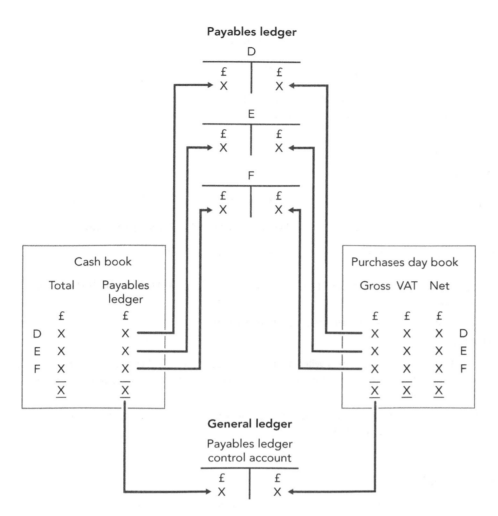

6 VAT control account

VAT control account: Used for all transactions related to VAT, and allows the business to identify clearly how much is owed to HMRC in respect of VAT in a period, or how much is due from them.

6.1 Recap of VAT

A further control account to consider is the **VAT control account**. Before we look at this account, it is useful to recap the principles of VAT seen in your earlier studies.

In the UK, VAT is administered and regulated by His Majesty's Revenue and Customs (HMRC). VAT is a tax on consumers that is collected on behalf of HMRC by VAT-registered businesses.

Not all businesses are registered for VAT. This means they cannot charge VAT on their sales or reclaim it on their purchases.

Those that are must (generally) charge 20% VAT on top of their sales and can reclaim VAT on their purchases.

 Illustration 3: VAT transactions

Example of VAT on sales

Net sales price	£100.00	Revenue retained by the business

 BPP

VAT @ 20%	£20.00	**Owed to HMRC**
Gross sales price	£120.00	Received from customer

In this illustration, the business retains £100.00 and records this as its sales revenue. When the VAT payment is due, it must hand over £20.00 to HMRC. It is, therefore, the customer who will have paid the VAT.

VAT charged on the sales price is referred to as **output tax**.

Example of VAT on purchases

Net purchase price	£40.00	Expense actually suffered by the business
VAT @ 20%	£8.00	**VAT a registered business can claim back**
Gross purchase price	£48.00	Amount paid to supplier

In this illustration, the business has to pay £48.00 but only suffers £40.00 as the VAT will be claimed back from HMRC.

VAT charged on the purchase price is referred to as **input tax**.

Payments to HMRC

At the end of the VAT period, the business will usually pay over to HMRC the excess of output tax over the input tax. In this illustration, the business would pay £12.00 to HMRC, being £20.00 output tax less £8.00 input tax.

If the business had paid more VAT to suppliers than it collected from customers, it would receive a refund from HMRC of the excess VAT paid.

6.2 Accounting for VAT

Output and input tax is accounted for at the same time as we record sales and purchases, but we must also account for payments of VAT owed to HMRC and refunds of VAT from them:

(a) The VAT amounts on sales and purchase invoices and credit notes, and on cash sales and purchases, are recorded in the day books and then totals are posted to the VAT control account.

(b) Payments to HMRC in respect of VAT owed are credited to the cash book and debited to the VAT control account.

(c) Receipts of VAT refunds from HMRC are debited to the cash book and credited to the VAT control account.

(d) The balance b/d on the VAT control account is the amount owed to (credit balance) or refundable by (debit balance) HMRC.

VAT control account

At the end of the VAT period the input tax is deducted from the output tax and the balance is paid to HMRC. The **VAT control account** is used to establish any balance due or reclaimable.

It is important to familiarise yourself with this account.

 ### Illustration 4: Preparing the VAT control account

A business has a credit balance b/d on 1 November 20XX of £3,000.

During November the following information regarding VAT is recorded:

Details	Amount £
VAT on sales	5,000

Details	Amount £
VAT on sales returns	500
VAT on cash sales	300
VAT on purchases	4,000
VAT on purchases returns	600
VAT on discounts allowed	200
VAT on discounts received	100
Bank payment to HMRC	2,800

Required

Prepare the VAT control account for November. Show the balance c/d at the end of the month and the balance b/d at the start of the next month.

Solution

VAT control account

Details	Amount £	Details	Amount £
Sales returns	500	Balance b/d	3,000
Purchases	4,000	Sales	5,000
Discounts allowed	200	Cash sales	300
Bank	2,800	Purchases returns	600
Balance c/d	1,500	Discounts received	100
	9,000		9,000
		Balance b/d	1,500

Explanation

Details	Explanation
Balance b/d	This is normally on the right-hand side of the VAT control account as it is a **liability**. Why? Well, in any profitable business the sale price exceeds the purchase price. Therefore VAT is owed to HMRC at the end of the VAT period (eg month/quarter).
Balance c/d	This is a **balancing figure** which enables the totals on both sides of the T-account to equal each other. It is usually a balancing figure on the left-hand side of the T-account.
Sales	When a business makes a sale it must pay the VAT collected on behalf of the customer to HMRC. Therefore a sale represents an **increase in liability**.

Details	Explanation
Cash sales	This works in the same way as credit sales, only the amounts involved will be smaller.
	There is still an **increase in liability** when a cash sale is made.
Purchases	When a business makes a purchase it can reclaim the VAT paid on that purchase from HMRC.
	Therefore a purchase represents a **decrease in liability**.
Sales returns	This has the opposite effect of a sale and is a **decrease in liability**.
	The VAT liability goes down as the product is returned.
	Therefore the VAT no longer needs to be paid to HMRC.
Purchases returns	This has the opposite effect of a purchase and is an **increase in liability**.
	The amount of VAT reclaimable has gone down as the business is returning the goods.
	Therefore the VAT cannot be reclaimed from HMRC.
Discounts allowed	If a credit customer takes advantage of a prompt payment discount, they owe less money to the business than is shown on the original sales invoice. Therefore the VAT due to HMRC decreases and so is entered as a debit on the VAT control account.
Discounts received	If a business pays promptly and takes advantage of a prompt payment discount, it will pay less money to the supplier than is shown on the original purchase invoice.
	Therefore the VAT reclaimable from HMRC decreases and so is entered as a credit on the VAT control account.
Bank	This is the payment made to HMRC or money received from them.

Assessment focus point

In the assessment you may well be required to prepare the VAT control account, either in T-account format or as a linear journal. Therefore you need to know whether items are entered on the debit or credit side of the control account.

Activity 3: VAT control account

The following is an extract from Michael's books of prime entry.

Totals for quarter				
		£		£
Sales day book			Purchases day book	
Net:		220,000	Net:	140,000
VAT:		44,000	VAT:	28,000
Gross:		264,000	Gross:	168,000

Totals for quarter			
	£		£
Sales returns day book		**Purchases returns day book**	
Net:	35,920	Net:	24,040
VAT:	7,184	VAT:	4,808
Gross:	43,104	Gross:	28,848
Discounts allowed day book		**Discounts received day book**	
Discount allowed:	2,400	Discount received:	1,200
VAT:	480	VAT:	240
Total:	2,880	Total:	1,440
Cash book			
Net cash sales:	54,000		
VAT:	10,800		
Gross cash sales:	64,800		

Required

(a) What will be the entries in the VAT control account to record the VAT transactions in the quarter?

Account name	Amount £	Debit ✓	Credit ✓
▼			
▼			
▼			
▼			
▼			
▼			
▼			

Picklist

- Bank
- Cash sales
- Discounts allowed
- Discounts received
- Purchases
- Purchases returns

 BPP

- Sales
- Sales returns
- VAT

The VAT return has been completed and shows an amount owing from HMRC of £24,184.

Required

(b) Is the VAT return correct?

	✓
Yes	
No	

Chapter summary

- The subsidiary receivables ledger and payables ledger and the receivables and payables control accounts are both prepared from information included in the books of prime entry.

- However, the subsidiary receivables ledger and payables ledger sit outside the general ledger. They enable businesses to see the amount owed by individual credit customers and the amount owed to credit suppliers.

- The receivables and payables ledger control accounts sit within the general ledger. They enable the business to see the total amount owed by credit customers and owed to credit suppliers.

- Reconciliations between the receivables ledger and the receivables ledger control account and the payables ledger and payables ledger control account are important and help to ensure the accounting records are free from error.

- The VAT control account is used for all transactions related to VAT, and allows the business to identify clearly how much is owed to HMRC in respect of VAT in a period, or how much is due from them.

Activity answers

Activity 1: Double entry (credit sales)

Account name	Amount £	Debit ✓	Credit ✓
Receivables ledger control	24,000	✓	
VAT	4,000		✓
Sales	20,000		✓

The receivables ledger control account is debited with the gross amount as the customer owes the full amount (VAT and net). The debit entry relates to the increase in assets.

A credit is made to the VAT account, as this is an increase in the amount owed to the tax authorities, and therefore the liability rises. A credit is also made to the sales account for the net amount, being the increase in income.

Activity 2: Double entry (credit purchases)

Account name	Amount £	Debit ✓	Credit ✓
Purchases	10,000	✓	
VAT	2,000	✓	
Payables ledger control	12,000		✓

A debit is made to purchases as this is an increase in expenses. The net amount is recorded in this account. A debit is also made to the VAT account as the money is reclaimable from the tax authorities, and therefore this is a reduction in the VAT liability.

A credit is made to the payables ledger control account as this is a liability (the gross amount will be paid to the supplier).

Activity 3: VAT control account

(a)

Account name	Amount £	Debit ✓	Credit ✓
Sales	44,000		✓
Sales returns	7,184	✓	
Purchases	28,000	✓	
Purchases returns	4,808		✓
Discounts allowed	480	✓	
Discounts received	240		✓
Cash sales	10,800		✓

The VAT relating to sales (both credit and cash sales) are included on the credit side of the VAT control account as this money is owed to the tax authorities.

The VAT on purchases is recorded on the debit side of the VAT control account as this money is reclaimable from the tax authorities. The debit is effectively a reduction in the liability.

The VAT on returns is included on the opposite side to the VAT recorded when the original transactions occurred, thereby cancelling out the VAT which arose on those sales or purchases.

(b) The correct answer is:

	✓
Yes	
No	✓

If the VAT control account is balanced off it shows a liability **due to** HMRC of £24,184. It is not due from HMRC.

Test your learning

1 In the month of March, a VAT-registered business receives sales returns of £1,800 from credit customers including VAT.

   Required

   What is the double entry to record this in the general ledger?

Account name		Amount	Debit	Credit
	▼	£	✓	✓
	▼			
	▼			

   Picklist

   - Bank
   - Payables ledger control
   - Purchases
   - Purchases returns
   - Receivables ledger control
   - Sales
   - Sales returns
   - VAT

2 In the month of April, a VAT-registered business returns goods it had purchased on credit costing £900 including VAT.

   Required

   What is the double entry to record this in the general ledger?

Account name		Amount	Debit	Credit
	▼	£	✓	✓
	▼			
	▼			

   Picklist

   - Bank
   - Payables ledger control
   - Purchases
   - Purchases returns
   - Receivables ledger control
   - Sales
   - Sales Returns
   - VAT

 BPP

3 DP is a small VAT-registered company that currently has only two credit customers. The opening balances on the receivables ledger accounts at the start of May 20XX were as follows:

	£
Virgo Partners	227.58
McGowan & Sons	552.73

The opening balance on the receivables ledger control account at the start of May was £780.31.

The sales day book and cash book – debit side for May are given below:

Sales day book

Date	Customer	Total	VAT	Net
		£	£	£
10 May	Virgo Partners	96.72	16.12	80.60
20 May	McGowan & Sons	595.08	99.18	495.90
30 May	Virgo Partners	214.44	35.74	178.70
		906.24	151.04	755.20

Cash book – debit side

Date	Details	Bank	Trade receivables
		£	£
4 May	Virgo Partners	117.38	117.38
15 May	McGowan & Sons	552.73	552.73
		670.11	670.11

Required

(1) Write up the receivables ledger control account for the month and the individual receivables ledger accounts.

(2) Agree the control account balance to the total of the subsidiary receivables ledger account balances at the end of the month.

General ledger

Receivables ledger control

Details		Amount	Details		Amount
		£			£
(1)	▼		(1)	▼	
(1)	▼		(1)	▼	
(1)	▼		(1)	▼	

Picklist 1

• Balance b/d

- Balance c/d
- Bank
- Receivables ledger
- Sales

Receivables ledger

Virgo Partners

Details		Amount	Details		Amount
		£			£
(2)	▼		(2)	▼	
(2)	▼		(2)	▼	
(2)	▼		(2)	▼	
(2)	▼		(2)	▼	

McGowan & Sons

Details		Amount	Details		Amount
		£			£
(2)	▼		(2)	▼	
(2)	▼		(2)	▼	
(2)	▼		(2)	▼	

Picklist 2

- Balance b/d
- Balance c/d
- Bank
- Invoice

Reconciliation

	Amount
	£
Receivables ledger control account balance as at 31 May	
Total of receivables ledger accounts as at 31 May	
Difference	

4 DP is a small VAT-registered business with two credit suppliers. The opening balances on its payables ledger accounts at the start of May were:

	£
Jenkins Suppliers	441.56

	£
Kilnfarm Paper	150.00

The opening balance on the payables ledger control account at the start of May was £591.56

The purchases day book and cash book – credit side for the period are given below:

Purchases day book

Date	Supplier	Total £	VAT £	Net £
5 May	Kilnfarm Paper	153.12	25.52	127.60
10 May	Jenkins Suppliers	219.96	36.66	183.30
20 May	Kilnfarm Paper	153.12	25.52	127.60
27 May	Jenkins Suppliers	451.32	75.22	376.10
		977.52	162.92	814.60

Cash book – credit side

Date	Details	Bank £	Trade payables £
10 May	Jenkins Suppliers	441.56	441.56
12 May	Kilnfarm Paper	150.00	150.00
27 May	Kilnfarm Paper	153.12	153.12
		744.68	744.68

Required

(1) Write up the payables ledger control account for May and the individual payables ledger accounts.

(2) Agree the control account balance at the end of May to the total of the list of individual balances in the subsidiary payables ledger.

General ledger

Payables ledger control

Details		Amount £	Details		Amount £
(1)	▼		(1)	▼	
(1)	▼		(1)	▼	
(1)	▼		(1)	▼	

Picklist 1

- Balance b/d
- Balance c/d
- Bank

- Purchases

Payables ledger

Jenkins Suppliers

Details		Amount £	Details		Amount £
(2) ▼			(2) ▼		
(2) ▼			(2) ▼		
(2) ▼			(2) ▼		
(2) ▼			(2) ▼		

Kilnfarm Paper

Details		Amount £	Details		Amount £
(2) ▼			(2) ▼		
(2) ▼			(2) ▼		
(2) ▼			(2) ▼		
(2) ▼			(2) ▼		

Picklist 2

- Balance b/d
- Balance c/d
- Bank
- Invoice

Reconciliation

	£
Payables ledger control account balance as at 31 May	
Total of payables ledger accounts as at 31 May	
Difference	

5 The following is an extract from a business's books of prime entry.

Totals for three-month period					
Sales day book					Purchases day book
Net:	£145,360		Net:		£71,840
VAT:	£29,072		VAT:		£14,368
Total:	£174.432		Total:		£86,208

Totals for three-month period				
Sales returns day book			**Purchases returns day book**	
Net:	£4,290		Net:	£2,440
VAT:	£858		VAT:	£488
Total:	£5,148		Total:	£2,928
Cash book				
Net cash sales:	£1,660			
VAT:	£332			
Total cash sales	£1,992			

Required

(a) Using the picklist to complete the details columns, make the required entries in the VAT control account to record the VAT transactions in the period.

VAT control

	Amount £			Amount £
▼		▼		
▼		▼		
▼		▼		

Picklist

- Cash sales
- Purchases
- Purchases returns
- Sales
- Sales returns

The VAT return has been completed and shows an amount owing from HMRC of £14,666.

Required

(b) Is the VAT return correct?

	✓
Yes	
No	

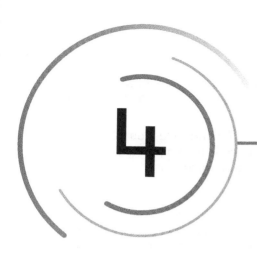

Preparing and reconciling control accounts

Learning outcomes

1	Use control accounts
1.1	Produce control accounts
1.1.1	Learners need to understand: the purpose of the receivables and payables ledger control accounts (part of the double-entry bookkeeping system)
1.1.2	the purpose of the VAT control account.
1.1.3	Learners need to be able to: prepare control accounts: • receivables ledger • payables ledger • VAT
1.1.4	total and balance control accounts: • balance carried down • balance brought down.
1.2	**Reconcile control accounts**
1.2.1	Learners need to understand: reasons for reconciling the receivables and payables ledger control accounts with the receivables and payables ledgers.
1.2.2	Learners need to be able to: total the balances of the individual receivables and payables ledger accounts: • receivables ledger debit/credit balances • payables ledger debit/credit balances
1.2.3	identify discrepancies between the receivables and payables ledger control accounts and the individual customer and supplier accounts
1.2.4	identify reasons for discrepancies between the receivables and payables ledger control accounts and the individual customer and supplier accounts.

Assessment context

Control accounts are a key part of the syllabus and an important part of the assessment. You will be asked to prepare the receivables or payables ledger control account and reconcile the control account with the relevant ledger account.

You may be asked to prepare control accounts in T-account format. Alternatively, you may have to present your answer in tabular format, by selecting an account name from a picklist, entering the correct amount, and then using tick marks to indicate debit and credit entries.

Qualification context

In the *Financial Accounting: Preparing Financial Statements* unit you could be required to identify the reasons why reconciliations are carried out as well as to determine the adjustments that may need to be made either to the control account balance and/or the individual receivables or payables ledger balance.

Business context

Businesses need to know the amount owed by their customers and to their suppliers at any given point in time. This encourages strong business relationships and efficient cash management.

Chapter overview

```
┌─────────────────────────────────────────────────────────┐
│        Preparing and reconciling control accounts        │
└─────────────────────────────────────────────────────────┘
```

Reconciliations

The RLCA and the RL and the PLCA and the PL are showing information from the same source (totals and individual accounts) so the overall balance should reconcile.

Receivables ledger control account

The total owed by all credit customers at a particular point in time

Payables ledger control account

The total owed to all credit suppliers at a particular point in time

Receivables ledger

A list of the amounts owed by each individual credit customer at a particular point in time

Payables ledger

A list of the amounts owed to each individual credit supplier at a particular point in time

Using control accounts

Credit control

- Credit control is the process of ensuring credit customers pay on a timely basis
- An aged receivables analysis enables the business to see the total amount owed by each customer and the age of the invoices

Irrecoverable debts

- If a credit customer cannot pay, the amount must be written off as an irrecoverable debt
- The journal to record an irrecoverable debt writeoff is:
  - Debit Irrecoverable debt expense
  - Debit VAT
  - Credit Receivables ledger control

Introduction

As we saw in the previous chapter, it is important to prepare receivables and payables control accounts. This enables the business to see the total amount due from credit customers and the total owed to credit suppliers at any point in time.

Individual receivables and payables ledgers are also maintained so that the business can see the amount owed by specific customers and due to specific suppliers. This ensures they can monitor the amount owed by customers and take action to recover outstanding balances where necessary. They can also retain supplier goodwill by settling amounts due within the agreed time period.

The control account balances will appear in the trial balance at the period end and, therefore, are ultimately included in the financial statements. Therefore accuracy is very important.

For this reason, control account reconciliations are key as it enables businesses to identify discrepancies and then take action to remedy them.

Receivables ledger control account reconciliation: An exercise that agrees the balance on the receivables ledger control account with the total of the list of balances in the receivables ledger.

Payables ledger control account reconciliation: An exercise that agrees the balance on the payables ledger control account with the total of the list of balances in the payables ledger.

1 Reasons for differences between the control account and the subsidiary ledgers

As was discussed in the previous chapter, if we add up the balances in the subsidiary receivables and payables ledgers, they should agree with the balances per the receivables and payables ledger control accounts.

If not, an error must have occurred at some point in the system.

In the assessment, having identified differences between the control account and respective ledger, you may be asked to identify the most likely reason(s) for the difference.

As you will have seen in the tasks above, there are many causes for the balance on the control accounts being different from the total of the ledger balances.

In general, differences are caused by:

- Only recording an item in the control account or ledger
- Over- or understating an item in the control account or ledger
- Duplicating an item in the control account or ledger
- Posting an item to the wrong side of the control account or ledger

To give some more specific examples:

The total balance of the receivables ledger will be higher than the receivables ledger control account if:

(a) A sales invoice has been duplicated in the receivables ledger

(b) A cash receipt from a credit customer has been omitted from the receivables ledger but recorded in the receivables ledger control account

(c) A sales returns credit note has been omitted from the receivables ledger but recorded in the receivables ledger control account.

The total balance of the receivables ledger control account will be higher than the receivables ledger if:

(a) Sales are recorded on the credit side of the receivables ledger but posted correctly to the control account

(b) The total column in the sales day book has been overstated

(c) The total column showing bank receipts from credit customers has been understated

(d) Discounts allowed have been posted twice in the receivables ledger but only once in the receivables ledger control account.

The total balance of the payables ledger will be higher than the payables ledger control account if:

(a) A purchases invoice has been duplicated in the payables ledger

(b) A cash payment to a credit supplier has been omitted from the payables ledger but is still included in the payables ledger control account

(c) A purchases returns credit note has been omitted from the payables ledger but recorded in the payables ledger control account

(d) Discounts received have been omitted from the payables ledger but recorded in the payables ledger control account.

The total balance of the payables ledger control account will be higher than the payables ledger if:

(a) Purchases are recorded on the debit side of the payables ledger

(b) The total column in the purchases day book has been overstated

(c) The total column showing bank payments to credit suppliers has been understated

(d) Goods returned have been entered twice in the payables ledger but only once in the payables ledger control account.

2 Assessment practice – control account reconciliations

Assessment focus point

In the assessment you could be asked to prepare a T-account or tabular format and calculate the balance to be carried down/brought down. You may also be asked to calculate specific balances (such as the balance c/d or balance b/d).

In the following activities we will practise assessment standard tasks.

Activity 1: Receivables ledger reconciliation – T-account format

This is a summary of transactions with credit customers during March 20XX.

Transactions	Amount
	£
Balance of receivables at 1 March 20XX	28,566
Goods sold on credit	15,477
Money received from credit customers	20,451
Discount allowed	233
Goods returned by credit customers	1,543

Required

(a) **Prepare a receivables ledger control account from the details shown above. Show clearly the balance carried down at 31 March (closing balance) and brought down at 1 April (opening balance).**

Receivables ledger control

Date 20XX	Details	Amount £	Date 20XX	Details	Amount £
	▼			▼	
	▼			▼	
	▼			▼	
	▼			▼	
	▼			▼	

Picklist

- Balance b/d
- Balance c/d
- Bank
- Discount allowed
- Sales
- Sales returns

The following balances were in the receivables ledger on 1 April 20XX.

	£
ABC Ltd	5,409
Beavers UK	2,385
Caratons & Sons	10,877
Elisons Ltd	1,234
George M & Co	789
Halisom Ltd	549
Walter Bambride	806

Required

(b) Reconcile the balances shown above with the receivables ledger control account balance you have calculated in part (a).

	Amount £
Receivables ledger control account balance as at 1 April 20XX	
Total of receivables ledger accounts as at 1 April 20XX	
Difference	

(c) What could explain the difference you calculated in (b)? Tick ONE option.

	✓
A sales invoice was duplicated in the receivables ledger control account.	
The bank payment was not entered in the receivables ledger control account.	
The total column of the sales day book was overstated.	
Discounts allowed were omitted from the receivables ledger accounts.	

Activity 2: Reconciling the receivables ledger with the receivables ledger control account

These are the accounts in the receivables ledger at 1 September.

Harry and Co

Details	Amount	£	Details	Amount	£
Balance b/f		10,100			

Smith and Sons

Details	Amount	£	Details	Amount	£
			Balance b/f		530

William Ltd

Details	Amount	£	Details	Amount	£
Balance b/f		16,650			

Bernards plc

Details	Amount	£	Details	Amount	£
Balance b/f		25,980			

Required

(a) What is the total of the balances in the receivables ledger on 1 September?

£ [   ]

The balance of the receivables ledger control account on 1 September is £51,560.

 BPP

Required

(b) What is the difference between the balance of the receivables ledger control account and the total of the balances in the receivables ledger you calculated in (a)?

£ [   ]

(c) Which TWO of the reasons below could explain the difference you calculated in (b)?

	✓
Goods returned may have been entered in the receivables ledger twice.	
Discounts allowed were entered on the debit side of the receivables ledger control account.	
Goods sold were entered twice in a customer's account in the receivables ledger.	
Goods returned were entered on the debit side of the receivables ledger control account.	
A cheque received was omitted from the customer's account in the receivables ledger.	
A cheque received was entered twice in a customer's account in the receivables ledger.	

Activity 3: Payables ledger reconciliation – T-account format

This is a summary of transactions with credit suppliers during March 20XX.

Transactions	Amount £
Balance of payables at 1 March 20XX	15,732
Goods bought on credit	15,567
Payments made to credit suppliers	13,731
Discount received	1,155
Goods returned to credit suppliers	2,251

Required

(a) Prepare a payables ledger control account from the details shown above. Show clearly the balance carried down at 31 March (closing balance) and brought down at 1 April (opening balance).

Payables ledger control

Date 20XX	Details	Amount £	Date 20XX	Details	Amount £
	▼			▼	
	▼			▼	
	▼			▼	

Date 20XX	Details	Amount £	Date 20XX	Details	Amount £
	▼			▼	
	▼			▼	

Picklist

- Balance b/d
- Balance c/d
- Bank
- Discount received
- Purchases
- Purchases returns

The following balances were in the payables ledger on 1 April 20XX.

Transactions	Amount £
Albats Ltd	2,345
Boleys UK	1,150
Carosel Ltd	1,157
Kasey & Sons	557
Latherwaite	789
Samsons Ltd	7,998
Tramptons UK	2,417

Required

(b) Reconcile the balances shown above with the payables ledger control account balance you have calculated in part (a).

	Amount £
Payables ledger control account balance as at 1 April 20XX	
Total of payables ledger accounts as at 1 April 20XX	
Difference	

(c) **What may have caused the difference between the control account and ledger balances?**
     Tick ONE option.

	✓
Goods returned may have been entered in the payables ledger twice.	
Goods returned may have been entered in the control account twice.	
Discounts received may have been entered in the payables ledger twice.	
Discounts received may have been entered in the control account twice.	

Activity 4: Payables ledger reconciliation

At the beginning of April the following balances were in the payables ledger:

Details	Amount £	Balances Debit/Credit
LBW Ltd	20,143	Credit
G Roe	18,402	Credit
L Mann	8,677	Credit
M Williams	1,850	Debit
H Hope	12,942	Credit
G Gold	847	Credit

Required

(a) **What should be the balance of the payables ledger control account in order for it to reconcile with the total of the balances in the payables ledger?**

	✓
Debit balance b/d on 1 April of £59,161	
Credit balance b/d on 1 April of £59,161	
Debit balance b/d on 1 April of £62,861	
Credit balance b/d on 1 April of £62,861	

(b) **Show whether the following are true or false.**

Statements	True ✓	False ✓
The payables ledger control account enables a business to identify how much is owed by credit customers in total.		
The total balances in the payables ledger should reconcile with the balances in the payables ledger control account.		

Statements	True ✓	False ✓
A debit balance in the payables ledger indicates a reduction in the total amount owed to credit suppliers.		

3 Credit control

One of the tasks of a credit controller (or credit control department) is to ensure that receivables pay on a timely basis and that any late payers are followed up promptly.

In order to follow up overdue invoices, the business must be able to identify overdue debts and determine how long customers take to pay.

A list of balances extracted from the receivables ledger will tell us how much each customer owes but not how long the invoices have been outstanding for. For that an aged trade receivables analysis is needed.

KEY TERM

Aged trade receivables analysis: A schedule showing, for each credit customer, how long the component parts of the balance have been unpaid.

Illustration 1: Credit control

Receivables ledger extract for Johnson Trading

Customer name	£
Bertrams	786
Florence	1,280
Quince	536
Titania	2,408
	5,010

The appropriate method of credit control, for example a polite letter or one threatening legal action, will depend on how overdue a debt has become.

From the example above we do not know if Florence always pays up and has only owed £1,280 for the past few days or if Titania Ltd has owed £2,408 for the past year.

In order to obtain sufficient information for credit control an aged trade receivables analysis must be prepared.

Aged trade receivables analysis for Johnson Trading

Customer name	Credit limit	Total balance	Up to 30 days	Up to 60 days	Up to 90 days	Over 90 days
	£	£	£	£	£	£
Bertrams	1,000	786	401	297	88	0
Florence	1,500	1,280	690	0	0	590
Quince	1,000	536	69	240	179	48

Customer name	Credit limit	Total balance	Up to 30 days	Up to 60 days	Up to 90 days	Over 90 days
	£	£	£	£	£	£
Titania	2,500	2,408	1,907	501	0	0
		5,010	3,067	1,038	267	638

This aged receivables listing analyses the balance owed by each customer according to the age of the invoice – ie how long it has been outstanding. This enables the appropriate action to be taken to collect the debt.

4 Irrecoverable debts

> **Irrecoverable debt:** A debt which it is believed will never be recovered.
>
> **Writing off:** Removing an irrecoverable debt from the ledger accounts.

As we know, the balance brought down in the receivables ledger control account is money due from customers. As it is something the business owns it represents an **asset**.

You are familiar with the concept that when a business sells on credit we record the invoice in the sales day book and that this is then posted to the main ledger using the following double entry:

Account name	Effect on elements	Debit ✔	Credit ✔
Receivables ledger control	Increase in asset	✔	
VAT	Increase in liability		✔
Sales	Increase in income		✔

The balance in the receivables ledger control account can remain as an asset in the accounting records as long as the business believes it is recoverable, ie that the credit customer will pay. However, whenever a business sells on credit, there is always a risk that the customer may not pay for the goods/services provided.

Consequently, the business must review the balances owed from credit customers and identify items that are at significant risk of non-payment. This review is performed regularly and, in particular, when the financial statements are prepared.

Accounting treatment

If a business believes a debt is definitely irrecoverable, then it is no longer an asset of the business and should be written off. The journal entry is:

Account name	Effect on elements	Debit ✔	Credit ✔
Irrecoverable debt expenses	Increase in expenses	✔	
VAT	Decrease in liability	✔	
Receivables ledger control	Decrease in asset		✔

The next activity enables you to practise this journal.

Activity 5: Irrecoverable debts

A credit customer, Geraldine, has ceased trading, owing Jessica Ltd £600 plus VAT at 20%.

Required

(a) Record the journal entries needed in the general ledger to write off the net amount and the VAT.

Account name		Amount	Debit	Credit
		£	✓	✓
	▼			
	▼			
	▼			

Another credit customer, DD Dayton, has ceased trading, owing Jessica Ltd £5,400 including VAT at 20%.

Required

(b) Record the journal entries needed in the general ledger to write off the net amount and the VAT.

Account name		Amount	Debit	Credit
		£	✓	✓
	▼			
	▼			
	▼			

Picklist

- Irrecoverable debt expenses
- Receivables ledger control
- Sales
- VAT

Assessment focus point

In the assessment you are likely to be required to write off an irrecoverable debt. Therefore, make sure you are able to record this journal in the general ledger.

Chapter summary

- If all of the entries in the general ledger are correctly made, then the totals of the closing balances on the subsidiary receivables and payables ledgers should agree with the balances on the relevant control accounts.

- If the entries in the general ledger and receivables and payables ledgers have not been properly made, then the total of these ledger balances will not agree with the balances on the control accounts – in which case the causes of the difference must be investigated.

- A receivables ledger control account reconciliation compares the balance on the receivables ledger control account with the total of the balances in the receivables ledger. Both are amended for any errors that have been made, so the balance and the total should be the same after putting through the amendments.

- A payables ledger control account reconciliation works in exactly the same way as the receivables ledger control account reconciliation, although all of the entries and balances are on the opposite sides.

- An aged trade receivables analysis is used to monitor how slowly customers are paying their debts, and to make decisions about how/when to chase for payment.

- The double entry for writing off an irrecoverable debt is to debit the irrecoverable debts expense account and the VAT control account, and credit the receivables ledger control account.

Activity answers

Activity 1: Receivables ledger reconciliation – T-account format

(a) Receivables ledger control

Date 20XX	Details	Amount £	Date 20XX	Details	Amount £
1 March	Balance b/d	28,566	31 March	Bank	20,451
31 March	Sales	15,477	31 March	Discount allowed	233
			31 March	Sales returns	1,543
			31 March	Balance c/d	21,816
		44,043			44,043
1 April	Balance b/d	21,816			

(b)

	Amount £
Receivables ledger control account balance as at 1 April 20XX	21,816
Total of receivables ledger accounts as at 1 April 20XX	22,049
Difference	233

(c) The correct answer is:

	✓
A sales invoice was duplicated in the receivables ledger control account.	
The bank payment was not entered in the receivables ledger control account.	
The total column of the sales day book was overstated.	
Discounts allowed were omitted from the receivables ledger accounts.	✓

The total of the subsidiary receivables ledger accounts is higher than the receivables ledger control account. Discounts allowed decrease the receivables ledger balance, and therefore omitting them from the receivables ledger accounts would cause this balance to be higher than the balance b/d in the receivables ledger control account. Therefore, Statement 4 is correct.

The other statements are incorrect. Duplicating a sales invoice in the receivables ledger control account would cause this balance to be higher than the receivables ledger accounts. Omitting the bank payment from the receivables ledger control account would also cause this balance to be higher than the total of the subsidiary receivables ledger accounts. Also, overstating the total column of the sales day book would cause the receivables ledger control account to be higher than the total of the subsidiary receivables ledger accounts.

Activity 2: Reconciling the receivables ledger with the receivables ledger control account

(a) £ 52,200

(b) £ 640

(c) The correct answers are:

	✓
Goods returned may have been entered in the receivables ledger twice.	
Discounts allowed were entered on the debit side of the receivables ledger control account.	
Goods sold were entered twice in a customer's account in the receivables ledger.	✓
Goods returned were entered on the debit side of the receivables ledger control account.	
A cheque received was omitted from the customer's account in the receivables ledger.	✓
A cheque received was entered twice in a customer's account in the receivables ledger.	

The total of the subsidiary receivables ledger balances is higher than the receivables ledger control account balance.

Statements 3 and 5 – this could be caused by a sales invoice being entered twice in a customer's account in the receivables ledger, as this would increase the total of the subsidiary receivables ledger balances. Also, a cheque received from a credit customer reduces the asset as the customer is settling an amount owed. Therefore, omitting it from a customer's account would cause the total of the subsidiary receivables ledger balance to be higher than the receivables ledger control account balance.

Statements 1 and 6 – duplicating goods returned and a cheque received from a credit customer in the receivables ledger would cause the total of the subsidiary receivables ledger balances to be lower than the control account, and hence they cannot be valid reasons here.

Statements 2 and 4 – including discounts allowed and goods returned on the debit side of the receivables ledger control account would cause this balance to be higher than the total of the subsidiary receivables ledger balance. This is not the case here; therefore, they do not explain the difference in this scenario.

Activity 3: Payables ledger reconciliation – T-account format

(a) Payables ledger control

Date 20XX	Details	Amount £	Date 20XX	Details	Amount £
31 March	Bank	13,731	1 March	Balance b/d	15,732
31 March	Discount received	1,155	31 March	Purchases	15,567
31 March	Purchases returns	2,251			
31 March	Balance c/d	14,162			
		31,299			31,299

 BPP

Date 20XX	Details	Amount £	Date 20XX	Details	Amount £
			1 April	Balance b/d	14,162

(b)

	Amount £
Payables ledger control account balance as at 1 April 20XX	14,162
Total of payables ledger accounts as at 1 April 20XX	16,413
Difference	2,251

(c) The correct answer is:

	✓
Goods returned may have been entered in the payables ledger twice.	
Goods returned may have been entered in the control account twice.	✓
Discounts received may have been entered in the payables ledger twice.	
Discounts received may have been entered in the control account twice.	

The total of the payables ledger control account is lower than the subsidiary payables ledger total by £2,251. Discounts received and goods returned both reduce the liability to credit suppliers, and therefore the duplication of the entry must have occurred in the payables ledger control account. The information in the scenario shows purchases returns as being £2,251; hence the difference is most likely to relate to the duplication of this item.

Activity 4: Payables ledger reconciliation

(a) The correct answer is:

	✓
Debit balance b/d on 1 April of £59,161	
Credit balance b/d on 1 April of £59,161	✓
Debit balance b/d on 1 April of £62,861	
Credit balance b/d on 1 April of £62,861	

(b) The correct answers are:

Statements	True ✓	False ✓
The payables ledger control account enables a business to identify how much is owed by credit customers in total.		✓
The total balances in the payables ledger should reconcile with the balances in the payables ledger control account.	✓	
A debit balance in the payables ledger indicates a reduction in the total amount owed to credit suppliers.	✓	

Statement 1 – the payables ledger control account enables a business to identify how much is owed by credit suppliers in total, not credit customers. Statements 2 and 3 are correct.

Activity 5: Irrecoverable debts

(a)

Account name	Amount	Debit	Credit
	£	✓	✓
Irrecoverable debt expenses	600	✓	
VAT	120	✓	
Receivables ledger control	720		✓

(b)

Account name	Amount	Debit	Credit
	£	✓	✓
Irrecoverable debt expenses	4,500	✓	
VAT	900	✓	
Receivables ledger control	5,400		✓

Note that scenario (a) is exclusive of the VAT, therefore the VAT is calculated as £600 × 20% = £120. The gross total posted to the receivables ledger control account is £600 + £120 = £720.

Whereas the VAT-inclusive amount is given in scenario (b). Therefore, the VAT is calculated as £5,400 × 20/120 = £900. The net total posted to the irrecoverable debt expense account is calculated as £5,400 − £900 = £4,500.

Test your learning

1 Indicate whether the following statement is true or false.

Statement	True ✓	False ✓
An aged receivables analysis is a schedule showing, for each credit customer, how long the component parts of the balance have been unpaid.		

2 The balance on a business's receivables ledger control account at the end of June was £40,500 and the total of the list of balances in the receivables ledger came to £40,250.

Required

Which of the following could explain the difference?

	✓
The sales day book was undercast by £250 on one page.	
An invoice for £250 was omitted from the receivables ledger account.	
A discount allowed to a customer of £250 was posted to the debit side of the receivables ledger account.	
Cash received of £250 was only posted to the receivables ledger control account.	

3 A credit customer, John & Co, has ceased trading, owing Hopkins £1,200 plus VAT at 20%.

Required

Record the journal entries needed in the general ledger to write off the net amount and the VAT.

Account name	Amount £	Debit ✓	Credit ✓
▼			
▼			
▼			

Picklist

- Irrecoverable debt expenses
- Receivables ledger control
- VAT

4 One of Grangemouth Ltd's credit customers, Markham & Co, has ceased trading, owing Grangemouth Ltd £1,290 plus VAT.

Required

Using the picklist, record the journal entries needed in the general ledger to write off the net amount and the VAT.

 BPP

Account name		Amount	Debit	Credit
		£	✓	✓
	▼			
	▼			
	▼			

Picklist

- Irrecoverable debts
- Receivables ledger control
- Sales
- VAT

5 The first two columns of the table in (a) show a summary of transactions with suppliers during the month of August.

Required

(a) **Show whether each entry will be a debit or credit in the payables ledger control account in the general ledger.**

Details	Amount	Debit	Credit
	£	✓	✓
Amount due to credit suppliers at 1 August	42,394		
Payments to credit suppliers	39,876		
Purchases on credit	31,243		
Purchases returned to credit suppliers	1,266		
Discounts received	501		

(b) **What will be the balance brought forward on 1 September on the above account?**

	✓
Debit £31,994	
Credit £31,994	
Debit £34,526	
Credit £34,526	
Debit £32,996	
Credit £32,996	

The following credit balances were in the payables ledger on 1 September.

	Amount
	£
Robinson Kate	8,239

	Amount £
Livesley Ltd	6,300
Townsend and Douglas	1,204
Miles Better Co	10,993
Strongarm Partners	4,375
Ambley Brothers	1,079

Required

(c) Reconcile the balances shown above with the payables ledger control account balance you have calculated in part (b).

	Amount £
Payables ledger control account balance as at 31 August	
Total of payables ledger accounts as at 31 August	
Difference	

(d) What may have caused the difference you calculated in part (c)?

	✓
A debit balance in the payables ledger may have been included as a credit balance when calculating the total of the list of balances.	
A credit balance in the payables ledger may have been included as a debit balance when calculating the total of the list of balances.	
A credit note may have been omitted from the purchase returns day book total.	
Discounts received may only have been entered in the payables ledger.	

5

The journal

Learning outcomes

3	**Use the journal**
3.1	**Produce journal entries to record bookkeeping transactions**
3.1.1	Learners need to understand:
	the purpose of the journal as a book of prime entry (manual and digital)
3.1.2	how the journal is used to record:
	• opening entries
	• irrecoverable debts written off
	• payroll transactions
	Learners need to be able to:
3.1.3	process journal entries to the general ledger accounts
3.1.4	record opening entries
3.1.5	record entries to write off irrecoverable debts:
	• record VAT where appropriate
	• calculate VAT from gross amounts
	• calculate VAT from net amounts
3.1.6	record entries for payroll transactions:
	• wages control account
	• gross pay
	• income tax
	• employer's and employees' National Insurance Contributions (NICs)
	• employer's and employees' pension
	• voluntary deductions.

Assessment context

We have been preparing journal entries since we first looked at double entry in *Introduction to Bookkeeping*. We now take this further by studying other transactions that businesses record by way of journal entry. In particular, preparing opening entries for a new business and payroll transactions are important areas of the syllabus.

Qualification context

In the Level 3 *Financial Accounting: Preparing Financial Statements* unit you will record journal entries for many accounting transactions, including items introduced in the unit such as accruals, prepayments and depreciation. In Level 4 *Drafting and Interpreting Financial Statements* you will process journals as you prepare the accounts.

Business context

Journal entries are necessary to prepare accurate, complete and reliable accounts which are used by company owners to assist with business decisions.

Chapter overview

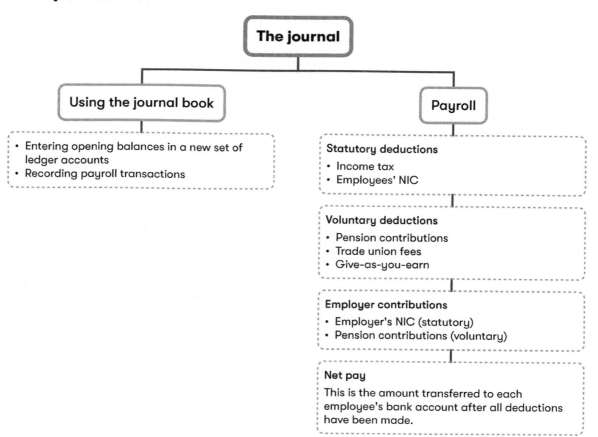

The journal

- Using the journal book
  - Entering opening balances in a new set of ledger accounts
  - Recording payroll transactions

- Payroll
  - **Statutory deductions**
    - Income tax
    - Employees' NIC
  - **Voluntary deductions**
    - Pension contributions
    - Trade union fees
    - Give-as-you-earn
  - **Employer contributions**
    - Employer's NIC (statutory)
    - Pension contributions (voluntary)
  - **Net pay**
    This is the amount transferred to each employee's bank account after all deductions have been made.

Introduction

Once the initial trial balance has been drawn up it will be reviewed to identify further adjustments that are needed before the accounts can be prepared.

These adjustments are recorded in a book of prime entry known as the **journal book**.

The journal book is used to record transactions that do not appear in any of the other books of prime entry, so they can then be posted to the ledgers.

For your assessment you need to be able to post journal entries to:

- Write off irrecoverable debts (seen in the previous chapter)
- Enter opening balances in a new set of ledger accounts
- Record payroll transactions
- Correct errors (studied in the next chapter).

The journal book serves the same purpose regardless of whether the business uses a manual accounting system or a digital accounting system.

When a digital accounting system is used:

- A journal entry is made in the journal book, together with the relevant nominal ledger account codes, and the affected nominal ledger balances are automatically updated
- Certain processes are automated, for example, if the transaction affects the receivables or payables ledger, assuming it is coded correctly, the subsidiary ledger and the related control account will both automatically be updated
- A journal entry can only be processed if the debit entry is equal to the credit entry (ie a journal that does not balance will not be accepted by the system).

Where a manual accounting system is used, the bookkeeper records the transaction in the journal book and then separately posts it from the journal book to the nominal ledger, and also to the subsidiary ledgers if appropriate.

1 Journal entries

> **Journal book:** The journal book is used to record transactions that do not appear in any of the other books of prime entry, so they can then be posted to the ledgers.
>
> **Journal entry:** A written instruction to the bookkeeper to make a double entry into the ledgers.

The journal consists of a series of journal entries. A **journal entry** is a written instruction to the bookkeeper to enter the transactions in the ledger.

Illustration 1: Journal entry

Journal number	0225	
Date	5 April 20XX	
Authorised by	D Fisher	
Account	**R Sanderson**	
Account name	**Debit (£)**	**Credit (£)**
Irrecoverable debts expense	700.00	
VAT control	140.00	
Receivables ledger control		840.00
Total	840.00	840.00

Journal number	0225		
Narrative: being to record an irrecoverable debt write-off in the nominal ledger.			

Points to note:

- The amounts to be entered in each ledger account are set out, and whether they are to be debited or credited.
- A total is calculated for debits and for credits, to check that the amounts are the same and, in turn, that the double entry is correct.

In your assessment, you would show this journal, as far as it affects the general ledger, as follows:

Account name	Amount	Debit	Credit
	£	✓	✓
Irrecoverable debts expense	700.00	✓	
VAT control	140.00	✓	
Receivables ledger control	840.00		✓

In the assessment, you may also need to prepare a journal for the receivables ledger:

Account name	Amount	Debit	Credit
	£	✓	✓
R Sanderson	840.00		✓

Assessment focus point

In the assessment you choose the account name from a given picklist of names, you enter the figure in the 'amount' column, and then you place a tick in the debit or credit column as appropriate. Note that you will **not** have to provide a narrative explanation of the journal in the assessment.

2 Journal to record opening entries for a new business

Journals are used to open the accounting records for new businesses.

Entering opening asset, liability and capital balances

To enter the business's assets, liabilities and capital in the new set of accounts:

- Asset accounts are entered as debit balances
- Liability and capital accounts are entered as credit balances.

 ### Illustration 2: Opening journal

Sarah Clifford is starting a business on 1 November 20XX with the following balances:

	£
Bank loan	22,000
Capital	10,000
Cash at bank	6,550

	£
Non-current assets	25,000
Petty cash	450

We need to create a journal to enter the appropriate opening balances in Sarah's accounts, as at 1 November 20XX.

To do this, first work through the list identifying balances as debits or credits.

Journal

Account name	Debit £	Credit £
Bank loan		22,000
Capital		10,000
Cash at bank	6,550	
Non-current assets	25,000	
Petty cash	450	
Totals	32,000	32,000

Next, the journal entry is posted to a new nominal ledger.

Bank loan

Details	Amount £	Details	Amount £
		Journal	22,000

Capital

Details	Amount £	Details	Amount £
		Journal	10,000

Cash at bank

Details	Amount £	Details	Amount £
Journal	6,550		

Non-current assets

Details	Amount £	Details	Amount £
Journal	25,000		

Petty cash

Details	Amount	Details	Amount
	£		£
Journal	450		

Assessment focus point

As you will see in the next activity, in your assessment you will be asked to record the opening journal entries for a new business. It is important to know whether the amounts in each account need to be included in the debit or credit columns.

Activity 1: Opening journal for a new business

Castle Timbers has started a new business, Castle Irons, and a new set of accounts are to be opened. A partially completed journal to record the opening entries is shown below.

Required

Record the journal entries needed in the accounts in the general ledger of Castle Irons to deal with the opening entries.

Account name	Amount	Debit	Credit
	£	✓	✓
Cash at bank	132,000		
Capital	100,000		
Motor vehicle	18,000		
Loan from bank	50,000		

3 Payroll

3.1 Introduction to payroll

Payroll transactions: Payments to employees in respect of salaries and wages.

Salaries and wages usually form a substantial part of a business's expenditure, especially in service organisations. However, salaries and wages expenditure does not arise in the same way as other cash and credit purchases.

The entries in the accounting system that are made in respect of salaries and wages are known as **payroll transactions**. To understand these, you need to have a basic understanding of the main statutory and voluntary transactions which are processed through payroll.

Assessment focus point

Note that for this assessment you do not need to know how to calculate tax; instead, the focus is on posting the journal entries to record payroll transactions.

KEY TERM

> **Gross Pay:** Gross pay is the salary or wages payable to an employee by the employer before any statutory or voluntary deductions.
>
> **Statutory deductions:** Deductions that must be made by the employer from an employee's pay in respect of income tax and employee's NIC.
>
> **Income tax:** A tax that is paid by individuals on all sources of income, including salary/wages.
>
> **National insurance contributions (employees' NIC):** A tax on employees' income deducted from gross pay.
>
> **His Majesty's Revenue and Customs (HMRC):** The UK government department responsible for collecting tax.
>
> **Voluntary deductions:** Non-statutory amounts deducted from employees' pay with their consent, eg give-as-you-earn (GAYE) and trade union subscriptions.
>
> **Pension contribution:** A form of voluntary deduction from employees, and a contribution from employers which is paid to the pension administrator to provide a pension for the employee on retirement.
>
> **Net pay:** The amount of the employee's wages actually paid to the employee, net of statutory and voluntary deductions.
>
> **National insurance contributions (employer's NIC):** An additional tax, suffered by the employer, based on an employee's gross pay.

Gross pay

Gross pay is the total amount that the employer owes the employee before any deductions have been made.

Statutory deductions

Income tax (pay-as-you-earn or PAYE) and **employees' national insurance contributions (NIC)** are known as statutory deductions from gross pay, because the law (statute) requires employers to make these deductions from individuals' salaries.

Employees pay their income tax under the PAYE system. This means that each time an employee is paid by their employer, the income tax for that period (eg monthly) is deducted from their wages by the employer. At regular intervals the employer then pays the income tax over to the tax collecting authority on the employees' behalf. In the UK the tax collecting authority is **His Majesty's Revenue & Customs (HMRC)**.

Employees must also pay employees' NIC to HMRC. NIC is just another form of tax, calculated differently from income tax. An individual employee's NIC are deducted from the employee's wages and paid over to HMRC, together with the employee's income tax.

Voluntary deductions

An employee may choose to have other (voluntary) deductions made from gross pay. These items can only be deducted from an employee's gross salary **if** the employer has the employee's written permission to do so.

For example, if an employee chooses to make pension contributions, this money is deducted from gross pay and transferred to a pension administrator to provide a pension for the employee on retirement. Other voluntary deductions include trade union fees and give-as-you-earn (GAYE).

Net pay

Once all deductions have been made, the amount paid to the employee is called net pay.

It is sometimes referred to as 'take home pay'.

Employer's national insurance contribution (statutory)

The employer is also required to pay an additional amount of NIC for each employee, known as the employer's NIC. This is yet another form of tax, but the difference is that it is only suffered by the employer. There is no deduction from the employee's gross pay for the employer's NIC. Employer's NIC is paid by the employer to HMRC.

Employer's pension contribution (voluntary)

The employer may make a voluntary contribution to the employee's pension. Again, this is in addition to the gross pay. Therefore, it increases the 'total cost' of employing individuals. However, it is not deducted from the gross pay.

Illustration 3: Payroll transactions

Let us suppose that Ian is employed by Southfield. He earns £48,000 a year which is paid monthly. This means that each month his gross pay is (£48,000/12) = £4,000.

Remember, gross pay is the amount an employee earns before any deductions are made.

Also, the gross amount also excludes any employer contributions made in addition to gross pay (such as employer's national insurance and pension contributions).

Statutory deductions

The payroll department of Southfield has calculated that the income tax due by Ian for this month is £770, and that his employees' NIC payment for the month should be £320.

Therefore, after statutory deductions have been made, so far Ian's monthly net pay is calculated as follows:

Item	Amount £	Paid by Southfield to:
Gross wages	4,000	
Income tax	(770)	HM Revenue and Customs
NIC	(320)	HM Revenue and Customs
Net pay	2,910	Ian

Voluntary deduction (pension contribution)

When Ian joined Southfield, it was agreed that each month he would pay £200 per month into the company pension scheme and Southfield would make a further contribution of £300 to the pension scheme.

Therefore, after statutory deductions and the employee's pension contribution have been made, so far Ian's monthly net pay is calculated as follows:

Item	Amount £	Paid by Southfield to:
Gross pay	4,000	
Income tax	(770)	HM Revenue and Customs
Employees' NIC	(320)	HM Revenue and Customs
Pension contribution	(200)	Pension scheme
Net pay	2,710	Ian

So, of the original gross wages of £4,000 per month, Ian only receives £2,710. However, the amount of income tax that he owed has been paid, as has the amount of NIC due from him, and he has also paid into his pension fund.

Employer's national insurance and employer's pension contributions

There are two further payments for Southfield to make. As we have seen, they have a statutory obligation to pay employer's national insurance contributions. This is £415 for Ian.

And they are making a voluntary contribution to Ian's pension of £300. In summary:

Type of payment	Amount	Paid by Southfield to:
	£	
Employer's NIC	415	HMRC
Employer's pension	300	Pension scheme

Therefore, the total cost to Southfield of employing Ian each month is:

Item	Amount
	£
Gross pay	4,000
Employer's NIC	415
Employer's pension	300
	4,715

3.2 Full cost of employing an employee

Where employer's pension contributions are made, the full cost of employing an employee is:

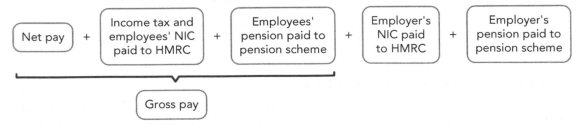

Therefore, gross pay plus employer's NIC plus employer's pension contribution is the cost of employing employees and what appears as the wages expense for the business.

3.3 Accounting for payroll

> **Wages control account:** A control account for recording payroll transactions. This is like any other control account and helps ensure that the double entry is made correctly.

Payroll is accounted for using the double entry bookkeeping rules that we are familiar with. There are, however, some new ledger (or T) accounts which are used for this purpose.

In this assessment, payroll transactions are recorded using a **wages control account**. Therefore, when payroll expenses occur, the liability is initially credited to this account.

Account name	Purpose
Wages control	This is like any other control account and helps ensure that the double entry is made correctly. All payroll liabilities are initially credited to this control account. They are subsequently transferred to the relevant nominal ledger account (such as HMRC, pension and bank).
Wages expense	This expense account shows the total cost to the business of employing someone (ie the gross salary **plus** the employer's NIC and, if applicable, the employer's pension contribution).

Account name	Purpose
HM Revenue and Customs	This liability account shows the amount of income tax and NIC owed to the tax authorities.
Pension	This liability account shows the amount of pension that must be paid over to the pension scheme. It will include both the employees' and employer's contributions.

Note that there may be other payable accounts if further voluntary deductions are made, say in respect of trade union fees and give-as-you-earn (GAYE).

There are a number of double entries to be made:

(a) **Gross pay is recorded:**

Account name	Debit	Credit
	✔	✔
Wages expense	✔	
Wages control		✔

(b) **Net pay is paid to employees:**

Account name	Debit	Credit
	✔	✔
Wages control	✔	
Bank		✔

(c) **Income tax and employees' NIC is allocated to the HM Revenue and Customs account:**

Account name	Debit	Credit
	✔	✔
Wages control	✔	
HM Revenue & Customs		✔

(d) **Employees' pension contributions are allocated to the pension account:**

Account name	Debit	Credit
	✔	✔
Wages control	✔	
Pension		✔

(e) **Employer's NIC is recorded:**

Account name	Debit	Credit
	✔	✔
Wages expense	✔	
Wages control		✔

(f) **Employer's NIC is transferred to the HMRC account:**

Account name	Debit	Credit
	✔	✔
Wages control	✔	
HM Revenue & Customs		✔

(g) **Employer's pension contributions are recorded:**

Account name	Debit	Credit
	✔	✔
Wages expense	✔	
Wages control		✔

(h) **Employer's pension contribution is transferred to the pension account:**

Account name	Debit	Credit
	✔	✔
Wages control	✔	
Pension		✔

Illustration 4: Accounting for payroll

We return to Ian's wages payment which is summarised below:

	£
Gross wages	4,000
Income tax	(770)
Employee's NIC	(320)
Employee's pension contribution	(200)
Net pay	2,710
Employer's NIC	415
Employer's pension contribution	300

The entries in the ledger accounts are as follows:

(a) **Gross pay of £4,000 is recorded:**

Wages expense

Details	Amount	Details	Amount
	£		£
Wages control (a)	4,000		

Wages control

Details	Amount	Details	Amount
	£		£
		Wages expense (a)	4,000

(b) **Net pay of £2,710 is paid to the employee:**

Wages control

Details	Amount	Details	Amount
	£		£
Bank (b)	2,710	Wages expense (a)	4,000

Bank

Details	Amount	Details	Amount
	£		£
		Wages control (b)	2,710

(c) **Income tax of £770 and employee's NIC of £320 is allocated to the HM Revenue & Customs account:**

Wages control

Details	Amount	Details	Amount
	£		£
Bank (b)	2,710	Wages expense (a)	4,000
HM Revenue and Customs (770 + 320) (c)	1,090		

HM Revenue & Customs

Details	Amount	Details	Amount
	£		£
		Wages control (c)	1,090

(d) **Employee's pension contribution of £200 is allocated to the pension account:**

Wages control

Details	Amount	Details	Amount
	£		£
Bank (b)	2,710	Wages expense (a)	4,000
HM Revenue and Customs (770 + 320) (c)	1,090		
Pension (d)	200		

Pension

Details	Amount £	Details	Amount £
		Wages control (d)	200

(e) **Employer's NIC of £415 is recorded and then;**

(f) **The liability is transferred to the HM Revenue and Customs account.**

Wages control

Details	Amount £	Details	Amount £
Bank (b)	2,710	Wages expense (a)	4,000
HM Revenue and Customs (c)	1,090	Wages expense (e)	415
Pension (d)	200		
HM Revenue and Customs (f)	415		

Wages expense

Details	Amount £	Details	Amount £
Wages control (a)	4,000		
Wages control (e)	415		

HM Revenue and Customs

Details	Amount £	Details	Amount £
		Wages control (c)	1,090
		Wages control (f)	415

(g) **Employer's pension contribution of £300 recorded and then;**

(h) **The liability is transferred to the pension account**

This is the final time we see the wages control account in this illustration. As a check that the double entry is correct, note that if we total the account there is no balance c/d. This suggests the payroll entries are correct.

Wages control

Details	Amount £	Details	Amount £
Bank (b)	2,710	Wages expense (a)	4,000
HM Revenue and Customs (c)	1,090	Wages expense (e)	415
Pension (d)	200	Wages expense (g)	300
HM Revenue and Customs (f)	415		
Pension (h)	300		

Details	Amount	Details	Amount
	£		£
	4,715		4,715

Wages expense

Details	Amount	Details	Amount
	£		£
Wages control (a)	4,000		
Wages control (e)	415		
Wages control (g)	300		

Pension

Details	Amount	Details	Amount
	£		£
		Wages control (d)	200
		Wages control (h)	300

The illustration suggests that accounting for payroll involves many journals. However, the essential principle is to:

- Debit the wages expense with the total cost (this is an expense, hence the debit entry)
- Credit the wages control account with the liability (an increase in liabilities is entered on the credit side of the T-account)
- Then, 'reallocate' amounts owed from the wages control account to the relevant liability account (HMRC, pension etc) and transfer the net pay to the individual (bank).

Assessment focus point / Exam success skills

In the exam you will record payroll journals in the ledger, using a wages control account. Therefore it is very important to learn the double entries required to enter each payroll transaction.

Activity 2: Accounting for payroll – HH Co

HH Co pays its employees by cheque every month and maintains a wages control account. A summary of last month's payroll transactions is shown below.

Item	Amount
	£
Gross pay	60,000
Employees' NI	2,000
Income tax	8,000
Employer's NI	4,000

Required

(a) Record the above information in the general ledger accounts.

General ledger

Wages expense

Details	Amount	Details	Amount
	£		£
▼		▼	
▼		▼	

Wages control

Details	Amount	Details	Amount
	£		£
▼		▼	
▼		▼	
▼		▼	
▼		▼	

Bank

Details	Amount	Details	Amount
	£		£
Balance b/f	100,000	▼	

HM Revenue and Customs

Details	Amount	Details	Amount
	£		£
▼		▼	
▼		▼	
▼		▼	

Picklist

- Bank
- HM Revenue and Customs
- Pension
- Wages control
- Wages expense

(b) Complete the following sentence.

The total cost to the business of employing staff is £ ☐

(c) Complete the following sentence.

The business owes £ [   ] to HM Revenue and Customs.

The above activity considers accounting for payroll transactions when only legal deductions occur. The next activity requires you to record payroll transactions with the additional consideration of **payroll contributions**.

Activity 3: Accounting for payroll – SMB Co

SMB Co pays its employees by cheque every month and maintains a wages control account. A summary of last month's payroll transactions is shown below.

Item	Amount £
Gross pay	9,452
Employees' NI	842
Income tax	1,305
Employees' pension contributions	140
Employer's NI	1,042

Required

(a) Record the wages expense

Account name	Amount £	Debit ✓	Credit ✓
▼			
▼			

(b) Record the HM Revenue and Customs liability

Account name	Amount £	Debit ✓	Credit ✓
▼			
▼			

(c) Record the net wages paid to the employees

Account name	Amount £	Debit ✓	Credit ✓
▼			
▼			

(d) Record the pension payable

Account name	Amount £	Debit ✓	Credit ✓
▼			
▼			

Picklist

- Bank
- Employees' NI
- Employer's NI
- HM Revenue and Customs
- Income tax
- Net wages
- Pension
- Wages control
- Wages expense

Activity 4: Accounting for payroll – Stanley

Stanley pays its employees by cheque every month and maintains a wages control account. A summary of last month's payroll transactions is shown below.

Item	Amount £
Gross pay	11,352
Employees' NI	901
Income tax	1,652
Employer's pension contributions	245
Employer's NI	1,241

Required

(a) Record the wages expense

Account name	Amount £	Debit ✓	Credit ✓
▼			
▼			

(b) Record the HM Revenue and Customs liability

Account name	Amount £	Debit ✓	Credit ✓
▼			

Account name		Amount £	Debit ✓	Credit ✓
▼				

(c) Record the net wages paid to the employees

Account name		Amount £	Debit ✓	Credit ✓
▼				
▼				

(d) Record the pension payable

Account name		Amount £	Debit ✓	Credit ✓
▼				
▼				

Picklist

- Bank
- Employees' NI
- Employer's NI
- HM Revenue and Customs
- Income tax
- Net wages
- Pension
- Wages control
- Wages expense

Chapter summary

- The journal book is used to record transactions that do not appear in any of the other books of prime entry, so they can then be posted to the ledgers. This includes:
  - Opening entries for a new business
  - Payroll transactions.
- When recording the opening entries for a new business, asset balances must be posted to the debit side of the ledger. Liability and capital balances are posted to the credit side of the ledger.
- The total payroll cost is the employees' gross pay plus employer's national insurance contributions (NIC) plus, where applicable, employer's pension contributions.
- Income tax and employees' NIC must be deducted from an employee's gross pay.
- Voluntary deductions may also be made, for example, employee pension contributions, trade union fees and give-as-you-earn (GAYE).
- Accounting for payroll involves the use of several nominal ledger accounts:
  - Wages control account
  - Wages expense account
  - HM Revenue and Customs account
  - Pension account
  - Other payable accounts if further voluntary deductions are made.

Activity answers

Activity 1: Opening journal for a new business

Account name	Amount	Debit	Credit
	£	✓	✓
Cash at bank	132,000	✓	
Capital	100,000		✓
Motor vehicle	18,000	✓	
Loan from bank	50,000		✓

Activity 2: Accounting for payroll – HH Co

(a) General ledger

Wages expense

Details	Amount	Details	Amount
	£		£
Wages control	60,000		
Wages control	4,000		

Wages control

Details	Amount	Details	Amount
	£		£
Bank	50,000	Wages expense	60,000
HM Revenue and Customs	8,000	Wages expense	4,000
HM Revenue and Customs	2,000		
HM Revenue and Customs	4,000		

Bank

Details	Amount	Details	Amount
	£		£
Balance b/f	100,000	Wages control	50,000

HM Revenue and Customs

Details	Amount	Details	Amount
	£		£
		Wages control	8,000

Details	Amount £	Details	Amount £
		Wages control	2,000
		Wages control	4,000

(b) The total cost to the business of employing staff is £ 64,000

The total cost is the gross salaries **plus** the employer's NIC. Therefore, £60,000 + £4,000 = £64,000.

(c) The business owes £ 14,000 to HM Revenue and Customs.

The business needs to pay the PAYE, employees' NIC and employer's NIC over to HMRC.

£8,000 + £2,000 + £4,000 = £14,000

Activity 3: Accounting for payroll – SMB Co

(a) Record the wages expense

Account name	Amount £	Debit ✓	Credit ✓
Wages expense	10,494	✓	
Wages control	10,494		✓

Working

£9,452 + £1,042 = £10,494

(b) Record the HMRC liability

Account name	Amount £	Debit ✓	Credit ✓
Wages control	3,189	✓	
HM Revenue and Customs	3,189		✓

Working

£842 + £1,305 + £1,042 = £3,189

(c) Record the net wages paid to the employees

Account name	Amount £	Debit ✓	Credit ✓
Wages control	7,165	✓	
Bank	7,165		✓

Working

£9,452 – £842 – £1,305 – £140 = £7,165

(d) Record the pension payable

Account name	Amount £	Debit ✓	Credit ✓
Wages control	140	✓	
Pension	140		✓

Activity 4: Accounting for payroll – Stanley

(a) Record the wages expense

Account name	Amount £	Debit ✓	Credit ✓
Wages expense	12,838	✓	
Wages control	12,838		✓

Working

£11,352 + £245 + £1,241 = £12,838

(b) Record the HM Revenue and Customs liability

Account name	Amount £	Debit ✓	Credit ✓
Wages control	3,794	✓	
HM Revenue and Customs	3,794		✓

Working

£901 + £1,652 + £1,241 = £3,794

(c) Record the net wages paid to the employees

Account name	Amount £	Debit ✓	Credit ✓
Wages control	8,799	✓	
Bank	8,799		✓

Working

£11,352 – £901 – £1,652 = £8,799

(d) Record the pension payable

Account name	Amount £	Debit ✓	Credit ✓
Wages control	245	✓	
Pension	245		✓

 BPP

Test your learning

1 A new business, Carswell & Sons, is opening a new set of accounts. A partially completed journal to record the opening entries is shown below.

Required

Record the journal entries needed in the accounts in the general ledger of Carswell & Sons to deal with the opening entries.

Account name	Amount	Debit	Credit
	£	✓	✓
Capital	28,000		
Cash at bank	21,000		
Loan from bank	5,000		
Machinery	12,000		

2 An employee earns a gross salary of £27,000 per year and is paid on a monthly basis. For the month of October, the payroll department has calculated an income tax deduction of £418.16 and NIC due of £189.00 from the employee and £274.50 from the employer.

Required

What is the employee's net pay?

£ [   ]

3 State whether the following deductions from gross pay are statutory or voluntary deductions:

	Statutory deduction ✓	Voluntary deduction ✓
Pension contributions		
Income tax		
Employee's NIC		
Trade union fees		

4 Indicate whether the following statements are true or false.

	True ✓	False ✓
Employer's NIC are deducted from gross pay.		
Employer's pension contributions are in addition to gross pay.		

5 A business pays its employees by BACS every month and maintains a wages control account. A summary of last month's payroll transactions is shown below:

Item	Amount £
Gross wages	12,756
Employer's NIC	1,020
Employees' NIC	765
Income tax	1,913
Trade union liability	100

Required

Using the picklist, record the journal entries needed in the general ledger to:

(a) Record the wages expense

Account name	Amount £	Debit ✓	Credit ✓
▼			
▼			

(b) Record the amount payable to HM Revenue and Customs

Account name	Amount £	Debit ✓	Credit ✓
▼			
▼			

(c) Record the net wages paid to the employees

Account name	Amount £	Debit ✓	Credit ✓
▼			
▼			

(d) Record the trade union liability

Account name	Amount £	Debit ✓	Credit ✓
▼			
▼			

Picklist

- Bank
- Employees' NIC
- Employer's NIC

- HM Revenue and Customs
- Income tax
- Net wages
- Trade union liability
- Wages control
- Wages expense

Learning outcomes

4.	Produce trial balances
4.1	Extract an initial trial balance
4.1.1	Learners need to know: how to use the general ledger to extract balances
4.1.2	the column to use in the trial balance: • debit • credit.
4.1.3	Learners need to be able to: transfer balances to the initial trial balance
4.1.4	total and balance the initial trial balance.

Assessment/Chapter context

Tasks are likely to give you a list of account balances and year-end figures, and ask you to correctly list them in the debit or credit column and total the columns. Accuracy is a key skill which is tested here.

Qualification context

In *Principles of Bookkeeping Controls* you have to prepare an initial trial balance and also process journal adjustments before the trial balance can be prepared. In Level 3 *Financial Accounting: Preparing Financial Statements* you will also be asked to process adjustments and produce a trial balance. In Level 4 *Drafting and Interpreting Financial Statements* you will prepare accounts from a trial balance.

Business context

The trial balance is used to summarise business transactions and from this the financial statements are prepared.

Chapter overview

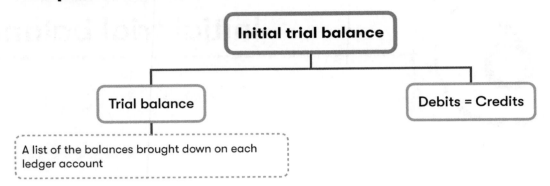

Initial trial balance

- **Trial balance**
  - A list of the balances brought down on each ledger account

- **Debits = Credits**

BPP

Introduction

In the *Introduction to Bookkeeping* course, we studied the accounting process.

Initially	Assorted transactions are recorded on financial documents (eg invoices)
Step 1	Input the transactions into the books of prime entry
Step 2	Process the transactions through the ledgers
Step 3	Generate output (eg summarise the information in the form of reports, trial balance, financial statements)

We have seen how business documents are categorised in the books of prime entry and how that information is then transferred from the books of prime entry and summarised in the general ledger. Now we need to extract a **trial balance** from the general ledger. The trial balance forms the basis of the financial statements.

1 The trial balance

A trial balance is drawn up by taking the **balance brought down** on each of the general ledger accounts and placing them in a **list**.

The list is divided into two columns, with one column for all the items with **debit balances** and another column for all the items with **credit balances**.

This is known as an **initial trial balance**.

> **Initial trial balance:** A list of all the debit and credit balances brought down on the ledger accounts.

Illustration 1: Trial balance

Trial balance as at 31 December 20XX

Account name	Debits £	Credits £
Bank	720	
Capital		500
Sales		2,200
Purchases	1,100	
Furniture	500	
Electricity	120	
Telephone	60	
Drawings	200	
Totals	**2,700**	**2,700**

The purpose of the trial balance is that it forms a check on the accuracy of the entries in the ledger accounts. **The total of the debit balances should equal the total of the credit balances.** If the **debits** in the trial balance **do not equal the credits** then this indicates that there has been an error in the double entry.

Only the ledger accounts in the **general ledger** are relevant to the preparation of the trial balance. The individual **receivables** and **payables ledger accounts** sit outside of the general ledger, and are not included in the trial balance.

Illustration 2: Initial trial balance

Below are Ben Charles's general ledger accounts.

GENERAL LEDGER

Bank

Details	Amount £	Details	Amount £
Capital	10,000	Purchases	1,000
Sales	1,500	Rent	600
Receivables ledger control	1,750	Non-current assets	1,000
		Stationery	200
		Drawings	500
		Payables ledger control	1,500
		Balance c/d	8,450
Total	13,250	Total	13,250
Balance b/d	8,450		

Capital

Details	Amount £	Details	Amount £
Balance c/d		Bank	10,000
Total	10,000	Total	10,000
		Balance b/d	10,000

Purchases

Details	Amount £	Details	Amount £
Bank	1,000		
Payables ledger control	2,000	Balance c/d	3,000
Total	3,000	Total	3,000
Balance b/d	3,000		

Payables ledger control

Details	Amount £	Details	Amount £
Bank	1,500	Purchases	2,000
Balance c/d	500		
Total	2,000	Total	2,000
		Balance b/d	500

Rent

Details	£	Details	£
Bank	600	Balance c/d	600
Total	600	Total	600
Balance b/d	600		

Sales

Details	£	Details	£
		Bank	1,500
Balance c/d	3,300	Receivables ledger control	1,800
Total	3,300	Total	3,300
		Balance b/d	3,300

Receivables ledger control

Details	£	Details	£
Sales	1,800	Bank	1,750
		Discount allowed	50
		Balance c/d	0
Total	1,800	Total	1,800
Balance b/d	0		

Non-current assets

Details	£	Details	£
Bank	1,000	Balance c/d	1,000
Total	1,000	Total	1,000
Balance b/d	1,000		

Stationery

Details	£	Details	£
Bank	200	Balance c/d	200
Total	200	Total	200

Details	£	Details	£
Balance b/d	200		

Drawings

Details	£	Details	£
Bank	500	Balance c/d	500
Total	500	Total	500
Balance b/d	500		

Discount allowed

Details	£	Details	£
Receivables ledger control	50	Balance c/d	50
Total	50	Total	50
Balance b/d	50		

Required

Now we will perform the next step in completing Ben Charles's accounts for the period by preparing a trial balance.

Solution

Step 1   List the balance brought down on each account as a debit or credit as appropriate.

	Debits £	Credits £
Bank	8,450	
Capital		10,000
Purchases	3,000	
Payables ledger control		500
Rent	600	
Sales		3,300
Receivables ledger control	0	
Non-current assets	1,000	
Stationery	200	
Drawings	500	
Discounts allowed	50	

Step 2   Total the debit column and the credit column and check that they are equal.

	Debits £	Credits £
Bank	8,450	

	Debits	Credits
	£	£
Capital		10,000
Purchases	3,000	
Payables ledger control		500
Rent	600	
Sales		3,300
Receivables ledger control	0	
Non-current assets	1,000	
Stationery	200	
Drawings	500	
Discounts allowed	50	
Totals	13,800	13,800

Activity 1: Initial trial balance

The general ledger T-accounts below are those that were prepared in Chapter 6 of the *Introduction to Bookkeeping* Course Book, for a company called Hampton. Using the balances brought down in the general ledger T-accounts, you are required to prepare a trial balance.

GENERAL LEDGER

Bank

Details	Amount	Details	Amount
	£		£
Capital	20,000	Purchases	250
		Rent	225
		Rates	135
		Balance c/d	19,390
	20,000		20,000
Balance b/d	19,390		

Capital

Details	Amount	Details	Amount
	£		£
Balance c/d	20,000	Bank	20,000
	20,000		20,000
		Balance b/d	20,000

Purchases

Details	Amount £	Details	Amount £
Bank	250		
Payables ledger control	450	Balance c/d	700
	700		700
Balance b/d	700		

Rent

Details	Amount £	Details	Amount £
Bank	225	Balance c/d	225
	225		225
Balance b/d	225		

Sales

Details	Amount £	Details	Amount £
		Cash	657
Balance c/d	1,407	Receivables ledger control	750
	1,407		1,407
		Balance b/d	1,407

Cash

Details	Amount £	Details	Amount £
Sales	657	Wages	75
		Balance c/d	582
	657		657
Balance b/d	582		

Rates

Details	Amount £	Details	Amount £
Bank	135	Balance c/d	135
	135		135
Balance b/d	135		

Receivables ledger control

Details	Amount £	Details	Amount £
Sales	750	Balance c/d	750
	750		750
Balance b/d	750		

Payables ledger control

Details	Amount £	Details	Amount £
Balance c/d	450	Purchases	450
	450		450
		Balance b/d	450

Wages

Details	Amount £	Details	Amount £
Cash	75	Balance c/d	75
	75		75
Balance b/d	75		

Required

Prepare the trial balance by placing the figures in the debit or credit column, as appropriate, and total each column.

Trial balance

Account name	Debit £	Credit £
Bank		
Capital		
Purchases		
Rent		
Sales		
Cash		
Rates		
Receivables ledger control		
Payables ledger control		
Wages		

Account name	Debit £	Credit £
Totals		

1.1 Balances to watch out for in your assessment

When you are given a set of general ledger T-accounts it is clear which side of the trial balance each balance should appear in: the same side as the **balance brought down** on the account.

However, in your assessment you will probably be given a list of balances and required to identify from their names whether they are debit or credit balances. You should watch out for the following, which students often get wrong.

Name of balance	Debit or credit balance?	Nature of balance
Inventory – of goods or materials held at any point in time	Debit	Asset
Bank overdraft	Credit	Liability
Bank **or** Cash **or** Petty cash	Debit	Asset
Loan	Credit	Liability
VAT owed to HMRC	Credit	Liability
VAT owed by HMRC	Debit	Asset
Capital	Credit	Capital
Drawings	Debit	Reduction in capital
Bank interest paid or bank charges	Debit	Expense
Bank interest received	Credit	Income

Activity 2: Preparing a trial balance

Below is a list of balances to be transferred to the trial balance as at 31 March 20XX. Each figure in the 'amount' column is the balance brought down on the T-account.

Required

Place the figures in the debit or credit column, as appropriate, and total each column.

Trial balance as at 31 March 20XX

Account name	Amount £	Debit £	Credit £
Motor vehicles	31,200		
Inventory	4,200		
Bank	18,260		
Receivables ledger control	8,800		
Payables ledger control	6,400		

Account name	Amount £	Debit £	Credit £
Capital	80,000		
Sales	130,000		
Sales returns	10,000		
Purchases	84,000		
Purchase returns	5,400		
Bank charges	200		
Discounts allowed	1,800		
Discounts received	1,200		
Wages and salaries	43,600		
Rent and rates	12,400		
Telephone	2,040		
Electricity	5,100		
Office expenses	1,400		
Totals			

Chapter summary

- A trial balance is prepared by listing all the debit balances brought down and credit balances brought down and checking the totals of these balances to ensure that they agree.
- The purpose of the trial balance is that it forms a check on the accuracy of the entries in the ledger accounts.

Activity answers

Activity 1: Initial trial balance

Trial balance

Account name	Debit £	Credit £
Bank	19,390	
Capital		20,000
Purchases	700	
Rent	225	
Sales		1,407
Cash	582	
Rates	135	
Receivables ledger control	750	
Payables ledger control		450
Wages	75	
Totals	**21,857**	**21,857**

> **Tutorial note.** Deciding whether a balance is a debit or credit balance is straightforward when you are given ledger accounts – if the balance b/d is on the debit side, you have a debit balance, and vice versa.

Activity 2: Preparing a trial balance

Trial balance as at 31 March 20XX

Account name	Amount £	Debit £	Credit £
Motor vehicles	31,200	31,200	
Inventory	4,200	4,200	
Bank	18,260	18,260	
Receivables ledger control	8,800	8,800	
Payables ledger control	6,400		6,400
Capital	80,000		80,000
Sales	130,000		130,000
Sales returns	10,000	10,000	
Purchases	84,000	84,000	
Purchase returns	5,400		5,400

 BPP

Account name	Amount £	Debit £	Credit £
Bank charges	200	200	
Discounts allowed	1,800	1,800	
Discounts received	1,200		1,200
Wages and salaries	43,600	43,600	
Rent and rates	12,400	12,400	
Telephone	2,040	2,040	
Electricity	5,100	5,100	
Office expenses	1,400	1,400	
Totals		**223,000**	**223,000**

Tutorial note. Preparing a trial balance from a list of balances requires a really good knowledge of debits and credits. Remember the DEAD CLIC mnemonic, and then work through each balance in turn applying DEAD CLIC. A good check of whether you have got the debits and credits right is whether or not the total of the debit column equals the total of the credit column.

Test your learning

1 Calculate and carry down the closing balances on each of the following accounts.

VAT account

Details	Amount £	Details	Amount £
Purchases	3,778	Balance b/f	2,116
Bank	2,116	Sales	6,145

Sales

Details	Amount £	Details	Amount £
		Balance b/f	57,226
		Receivables ledger control	42,895

Receivables ledger control

Details	Amount £	Details	Amount £
Balance b/f	4,689	Bank	21,505
Sales	23,512	Discounts allowed	2,019

Payables ledger control

Details	Amount £	Details	Amount £
Purchase returns	1,334	Balance b/f	2,864
Bank	13,446	Purchases	14,552
Discounts received	662		

Details	Amount £	Details	Amount £

2 Indicate whether each of the following balances would be shown as a debit balance or a credit balance in the trial balance.

	Amount £	Debit balance ✓	Credit balance ✓
Discounts allowed	1,335		
Discounts received	1,013		
Purchase returns	4,175		
Sales returns	6,078		
Bank interest received	328		
Bank charges	163		

3 Given below are the balances on the ledger accounts of Thames Traders at 30 November 20XX. Prepare the trial balance as at 30 November 20XX, including totals.

	£	Debit £	Credit £
Motor vehicles	64,000		
Office equipment	21,200		
Sales	238,000		
Purchases	164,000		
Cash	300		
Bank overdraft	1,080		
Petty cash	30		
Capital	55,000		
Sales returns	4,700		
Purchase returns	3,600		
Receivables ledger control	35,500		
Payables ledger control	30,100		
VAT (owed to HMRC)	12,950		
Telephone	1,600		
Electricity	2,800		
Wages	62,100		

	£	Debit £	Credit £
Loan from bank	30,000		
Discounts allowed	6,400		
Discounts received	3,900		
Rent expense	12,000		
Totals			

4 Below is a list of balances to be transferred to the trial balance as at 30 June.

Required

Place the figures in the debit or credit column, as appropriate, and total each column.

Account name	Amount £	Debit £	Credit £
Advertising	3,238		
Bank overdraft	27,511		
Capital	40,846		
Cash	689		
Discount allowed	4,416		
Discount received	2,880		
Hotel expenses	2,938		
Inventory	46,668		
Loan from bank	39,600		
Miscellaneous expenses	3,989		
Motor expenses	7,087		
Motor vehicles	63,120		
Payables ledger control	110,846		
Petty cash	720		
Purchases	634,529		
Purchase returns	1,618		
Receivables ledger control	405,000		
Rent and rates	19,200		
Sales	1,051,687		
Sales returns	11,184		
Stationery	5,880		

 BPP

Account name	Amount £	Debit £	Credit £
Subscriptions	864		
Telephone	3,838		
VAT (owing to HMRC)	63,650		
Wages	125,278		
Totals			

5   Below are two ledger accounts and a partially completed trial balance.

Cash

Details	£	Details	£
Balance b/f	1,000.00	Cash payments	720.00
Cash receipts	240.00	Balance c/d	520.00
	1,240.00		1,240.00
Balance b/d	520.00		

VAT account

Details	£	Details	£
Sales returns	44.00	Balance b/f	1,500.00
Purchases	1,108.00	Sales	280.00
Cash	120.00	Cash	40.00
Balance c/d	640.00	Purchase returns	92.00
	1,912.00		1,912.00
		Balance b/d	640.00

Required

Complete the trial balance by:

* Transferring the balances of the two general ledger accounts to the debit or credit column of the trial balance
* Entering the amounts shown against each of the other names into the debit or credit column of the trial balance
* Totalling both columns of the trial balance.

Trial balance

Account name	Amount £	Debit £	Credit £
Cash			
Bank	9,320.00		
Receivables ledger control	10,000.00		

 BPP

Account name	Amount £	Debit £	Credit £
Sales	21,650.00		
Sales returns	230.00		
VAT			
Discounts allowed	40.00		
Payables ledger control	2,500.00		
Purchases	6,300.00		
Purchase returns	480.00		
Discounts received	140.00		
Capital	1,000.00		

7

Errors and the trial balance

Learning outcomes

3	**Use the journal**
3.2	**Produce journal entries to correct errors not disclosed by the trial balance**
3.2.2	types of errors not disclosed by the trial balance (manual and digital): • error of commission • error of omission • error of original entry • error of principle • reversal of entries • compensating errors.
3.2.3	Learners need to be able to: correct errors using the journal
3.3	**Produce journal entries to correct errors disclosed by the trial balance**
3.3.1	Learners need to understand: the purpose of a suspense account
3.3.2	Learners need to be able to: open a suspense account
3.3.3	correct errors and clear the suspense account using the journal.
4.	**Produce trial balances**
4.2	**Redraft the trial balance following adjustments**
4.2.1	Learners need to be able to: recalculate the balance of a general ledger account following journal entries
4.2.2	complete a trial balance from adjusted and unadjusted balances
4.2.3	balance the adjusted trial balance: total debit and credit columns.

Assessment context

You will be given details of transactions which have been recorded incorrectly. You will be required to enter journals to remove the incorrect entry, record the correct entry and, where relevant, clear the suspense account. Some tasks will ask you to redraft the trial balance following the correction of errors.

Qualification context

In the *Financial Accounting: Preparing Financial Statements* unit you may be asked to identify the cause of imbalances in the trial balance and take appropriate action to remedy them.

Business context

All businesses must be able to identify errors, and correct them in a timely, appropriate manner in order to prepare accurate, complete financial statements.

Chapter overview

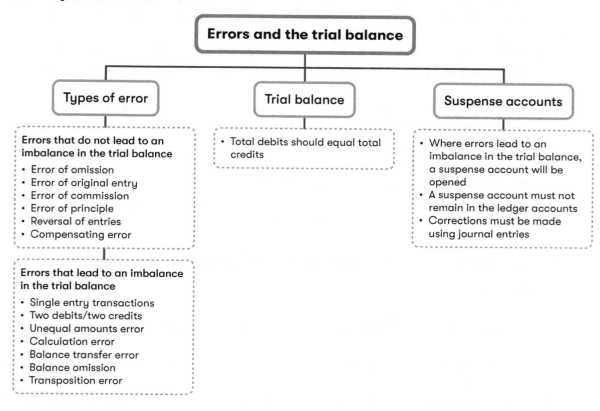

Errors and the trial balance

Types of error

Errors that do not lead to an imbalance in the trial balance
- Error of omission
- Error of original entry
- Error of commission
- Error of principle
- Reversal of entries
- Compensating error

Errors that lead to an imbalance in the trial balance
- Single entry transactions
- Two debits/two credits
- Unequal amounts error
- Calculation error
- Balance transfer error
- Balance omission
- Transposition error

Trial balance
- Total debits should equal total credits

Suspense accounts
- Where errors lead to an imbalance in the trial balance, a suspense account will be opened
- A suspense account must not remain in the ledger accounts
- Corrections must be made using journal entries

 BPP

Introduction

When the bookkeeper is preparing to draft the financial statements they will first prepare an initial trial balance. A trial balance is a list of the debit and credit balances on each of the general ledger accounts.

When totalled, the sum of the debit column should equal the sum of the credit column.

If the debits in the trial balance do not equal the credits then this means that an error has been made.

If the debit and credit columns balance, this is a good sign. However, it could mask the fact that an error has been made when making entries in the ledger accounts.

Therefore, we can distinguish between:

- Errors that do not lead to an imbalance on the trial balance
- Errors that lead to an imbalance on the trial balance.

It is important to understand the different types of errors that can arise and, most importantly, the journal entries required to correct them.

1 Errors that do not lead to an imbalance in the trial balance

KEY TERM

Error of omission: Both the debit and credit entries have been omitted from the ledger accounts.

Error of original entry: Both the debit and credit entries in the ledgers have been made at the wrong amount.

Error of commission: The double entry is arithmetically correct but one of the entries has been made to the wrong account, though an account of the correct type.

Error of principle: The double entry is arithmetically correct but one of the entries has been to the wrong type of account.

Reversal of entries: The debit and credit entries have been reversed in the ledger accounts.

Compensating error: Two (or more) separate errors have been made that completely cancel each other out.

Errors that do not lead to an imbalance in the trial balance will not be disclosed by the trial balance, regardless of whether the business uses a manual accounting system or a digital accounting system.

Assessment focus point

For assessment purposes, these can be summarised as:

- Error of omission
- Error of original entry
- Error of commission
- Error of principle
- Reversal of entries
- Compensating error

Let us consider each of the above types of error in turn. This will be explained through illustrations.

Error of omission

The entry is completely omitted from the ledger accounts.

Illustration 1: Error of omission

A payment for electricity of £80 was not recorded.

Required

(a) What was the original entry?

(b) What should the entry have been?

(c) Prepare journal entries to record this transaction.

Solution

(a) Original entry

Account name	Debit £	Credit £
Electricity	nil	
Bank		nil

(b) The entry should have been:

Account name	Debit £	Credit £
Electricity	80	
Bank		80

(c) Journal entries to record the transaction

Account name	Debit £	Credit £
Electricity	80	
Bank		80

Error of original entry

An entry has been made so that debits = credits but the amount is incorrect.

Illustration 2: Error of original entry

A payment of £520 from a credit customer is recorded as £250.

Required

(a) What was the original entry?

(b) What should the entry have been?

(c) Record the journal to:

    (1) Remove the incorrect entries

    (2) Record the correct entries

Solution

(a) Original entry

Account name	Debit £	Credit £
Bank	250	
Receivables ledger control		250

(b) Entry should have been:

Account name	Debit £	Credit £
Bank	520	
Receivables ledger control		520

(c) Remove the incorrect entries

Account name	Debit £	Credit £
Receivables ledger control	250	
Bank		250

Record the correct entries

Account name	Debit £	Credit £
Bank	520	
Receivables ledger control		520

Note that in practice errors are often corrected by posting the difference to the account affected. However, in the assessment you are required to first remove the incorrect entry and then record the correct entry, as is shown here.

Error of commission

The double entry is arithmetically correct but a wrong account of the same type has been used.

 Illustration 3: Error of commission

The wages and salaries expense account is incorrectly debited with a rent expense of £100.

Required

(a) What was the original entry?

(b) What should the entry have been?

(c) Prepare journal entries to:

  (1) Remove the incorrect entry

  (2) Record the correct entry

Solution

(a) Original entry

Account name	Debit £	Credit £
Wages and salaries expense	100	
Bank		100

(b) Entry should have been:

Account name	Debit £	Credit £
Rent	100	
Bank		100

(c) Remove the incorrect entry

Account name	Debit £	Credit £
Wages and salaries expense		100

Record the correct entry

Account name	Debit £	Credit £
Rent	100	

Error of principle

This is similar to an error of commission, but this time the wrong type of account has been used. A posting is made to a statement of profit or loss (SPL) account instead of a statement of financial position (SOFP) account or vice versa.

When the company accounts are prepared, both the SPL and SOFP will be incorrect (unless the error is detected and corrected).

Illustration 4: Error of principle

A motor vehicle petrol expense of £40 is debited to the non-current asset motor vehicles account instead of being expensed to the statement of profit or loss.

Required

(a) What was the original entry?

(b) What should the entry have been?

(c) Prepare journal entries to:

(1) Remove the incorrect entry

(2) Record the correct entry

Solution

(a) Original entry

Account name	Debit £	Credit £
Motor vehicles (SOFP)	40	
Bank		40

(b) Entry should have been

Account name	Debit £	Credit £
Motor vehicles expense (SPL)	40	
Bank		40

(c) Remove the incorrect entry

Account name	Debit £	Credit £
Motor vehicles (SOFP)		40

Record the correct entry

Account name	Debit £	Credit £
Motor vehicles expense (SPL)	40	

Reversal of entries

The debit and credit entries are on the wrong side of the respective accounts.

Illustration 5: Reversal of entries

The entries to record a sale on credit of £160 were included on the wrong side of the respective accounts.

Required

(a) What was the original entry?

(b) What should the entry have been?

(c) Prepare journal entries to:

    (1) Remove the incorrect entries

    (2) Record the correct entries

Solution

(a) Original entry

Account name	Debit £	Credit £
Sales	160	
Receivables ledger control		160

(b) Entry should have been:

Account name	Debit £	Credit £
Receivables ledger control	160	
Sales		160

(c) Remove the incorrect entries

Account name	Debit £	Credit £
Sales		160
Receivables ledger control	160	

Record the correct entries

Account name	Debit £	Credit £
Receivables ledger control	160	
Sales		160

Compensating error

This is where two errors are made which exactly cancel each other out. The errors are unrelated but the fact that they both occurred will mean that there is no imbalance in the trial balance to help identify them. (These are rare in practice.)

 ## Illustration 6: Compensating error

The receivables ledger control account was incorrectly debited with £4,100 in respect of a sales transaction. The correct amount of £4,000 was credited to the sales account.

The purchases returns account was incorrectly credited with £1,600 in respect of a purchases returns transaction. The correct amount of £1,500 was debited to the payables ledger control account.

Required

(a) What was the original entry?

(b) What should the entry have been?

(c) Prepare journal entries to:

(1) Remove the incorrect entries

(2) Record the correct entries

 BPP

Solution

(a) Original entry

Account name	Debit £	Credit £
Receivables ledger control	4,100	
Sales		4,000
Payables ledger control	1,500	
Purchases returns		1,600

(b) Entry should have been:

Account name	Debit £	Credit £
Receivables ledger control	4,000	
Sales		4,000
Payables ledger control	1,500	
Purchases returns		1,500

(c) Journal to remove the incorrect entries

Account name	Debit £	Credit £
Receivables ledger control		4,100
Purchases returns	1,600	

Journal to record the correct entries

Account name	Debit £	Credit £
Receivables ledger control	4,000	
Purchases returns		1,500

2 Errors that lead to an imbalance in the trial balance

Single entry transactions: Only one side of the double entry has been made.

Two debits/two credits error: Instead of a debit and a credit entry, either two debits or two credits have been made.

Unequal amounts error: Debit and credit entries have been made for different amounts.

Calculation error: A mistake is made in calculating the balance on a ledger account.

Balance transfer error: A balance on a general ledger account is transferred incorrectly into the trial balance.

Balance omission: A ledger account balance has been left out of the trial balance completely.

Transposition error: The digits in a number are transposed (swapped round).

Suspense account: An account opened in order to make the balances on a trial balance equal while the reason for the imbalance is discovered and corrected.

Errors that lead to an imbalance in the trial balance can be summarised as:
- Single entry transactions
- Two debits/two credits
- Unequal amounts error
- Calculation error
- Balance transfer error
- Balance omission
- Transposition error

Where these errors occur, in the initial trial balance total debits will not equal total credits. Therefore, a **suspense account** is opened to make the trial balance totals equal.

The suspense account must **not** remain in the ledger accounts. The reasons for the imbalance on the trial balance must be investigated and corrections made using journal entries. Once the corrections have been put through, the suspense account will be cleared to a balance of zero.

The steps to follow to identify and correct errors are to:
- Identify what the incorrect double entry was
- Determine what the correct double entry should have been
- Prepare the journal entries to:
  - Remove the incorrect entry
  - Record the correct entry
  - Remove the suspense account balance.

Most digital accounting systems will only accept bookkeeping entries where the debit entry is equal to the credit entry, and vice versa. Imbalances can arise in a digital accounting system where a business imports financial data from other systems to the accounting module. However, the steps to identify and correct errors follow the same principles as in a manual accounting system.

Assessment focus point

As mentioned above, in practice it is also possible to make net journal entries, which reverse and correct only the incorrect original entries, leaving the parts of the entries that were made correctly the first time unaffected. In the AAT assessment, however, you need to follow the 'reverse and correct' approach, as we see in the study material.

The illustration below shows several errors which have led to an imbalance in the trial balance. At the start of the illustration the suspense account is opened. The journals required to correct the errors are then processed and by the end of the illustration, the balance on the suspense account has been cleared.

This is longer than an assessment-standard task and demonstrates the principles you need to understand with regard to clearing a suspense account balance.

Note that for each of the examples, when we ask 'What was the original entry?', we are considering the journals that would have been made by the bookkeeper. If there is an imbalance in the journal entries, by default the balancing figure (β) will go to the suspense account.

Illustration 7: Errors that lead to an imbalance in the trial balance

A business drafted its initial trial balance and found the totals of the debit and credit columns were as follows:

Account name	Debit £	Credit £
Trial balance totals (initial)	150,500	160,000

The difference of £9,500 is initially dealt with by opening a suspense account to create a balanced trial balance.

Account name	Debit £	Credit £
Trial balance totals (initial)	150,500	160,000
Suspense	9,500	
Trial balance totals	160,000	160,000

The trial balance now balances but there is also a temporary new general ledger account, the suspense account, with a debit balance.

Suspense

Details	Amount £	Details	Amount £
Balance b/f	9,500		

The following errors are identified:

Single entry transactions

One side of the double entry has been made (eg the debit and not the credit).

Example (i)

A wages and salaries transaction of £4,482 is only recorded in the wages and salaries control account. The entry to the wages and salaries expense account is omitted.

What was the original entry?

Account name	Debit £	Credit £
Wages and salaries expense	0	
Suspense β	4,482	
Wages and salaries control		4,482

What should the entry have been?

Account name	Debit £	Credit £
Wages and salaries expense	4,482	
Wages and salaries control		4,482

Prepare journal entries to:

(a) Record the correct entry

Account name	Debit £	Credit £
Wages and salaries expense	4,482	

(b) Record the entry to remove the suspense account balance

Account name	Debit £	Credit £
Suspense		4,482

Two debits/two credits

Both accounts have been posted with debit entries or both accounts have been posted with credit entries.

Example (ii)

An electricity payment of £2,500 is credited to both general ledger accounts.

What was the original entry?

Account name	Debit £	Credit £
Suspense β	5,000	
Electricity expense		2,500
Bank		2,500

What should the entry have been?

Account name	Debit £	Credit £
Electricity expense	2,500	
Bank		2,500

Prepare journal entries to:

(a) Remove the incorrect entry

Account name	Debit £	Credit £
Electricity expense	2,500	

(b) Record the correct entry

Account name	Debit £	Credit £
Electricity expense	2,500	

(c) Remove the suspense account balance

Account name	Debit £	Credit £
Suspense		5,000

Unequal amounts error

One side of the double entry is made accurately but an error is made in the other side.

Example (iii)

A rent payment was correctly posted to the rent expense account as £1,100 but incorrectly posted to the bank account as £1,000.

What was the original entry?

Account name	Debit £	Credit £
Rent expense	1,100	
Bank		1,000
Suspense β		100

What should the entry have been?

Account name	Debit £	Credit £
Rent expense	1,100	
Bank		1,100

Prepare journal entries to:

(a) Remove the incorrect entry

Account name	Debit £	Credit £
Bank	1,000	

(b) Record the correct entry

Account name	Debit £	Credit £
Bank		1,100

(c) Remove the suspense account balance

Account name	Debit £	Credit £
Suspense	100	

Calculation error

A mistake is made when calculating the balance on a ledger account.

Example (iv)

The receivables ledger control account has not been correctly balanced. It should show £1,200 on the receivables ledger control account instead of £700. The corresponding credit entries were correctly included in the trial balance.

What was the original entry?

Account name	Debit £	Credit £
Receivables ledger control	700	
Suspense β	500	

What should the entry have been?

Account name	Debit £	Credit £
Receivables ledger control	1,200	

Prepare journal entries to:

(a) Remove the incorrect entry

Account name	Debit £	Credit £
Receivables ledger control		700

(b) Record the correct entry

Account name	Debit £	Credit £
Receivables ledger control	1,200	

(c) Remove the suspense account balance

Account name	Debit £	Credit £
Suspense		500

Balance transfer error

A balance on a general ledger account is transferred incorrectly into the trial balance.

Example (v)

A balance on the petty cash account was included in the trial balance as £600. It should have been £550. The corresponding credit entries were correctly included in the trial balance.

What was the original entry?

Account name	Debit £	Credit £
Petty cash account in the TB	600	
Suspense β		50

What should the entry have been?

Account name	Debit £	Credit £
Petty cash account in the TB	550	

Prepare journal entries to:

(a) Remove the incorrect entry

Account name	Debit £	Credit £
Petty cash account in the TB		600

(b) Record the correct entry

Account name	Debit £	Credit £
Petty cash account in the TB	550	

(c) Remove the suspense account balance

Account name	Debit £	Credit £
Suspense	50	

Balance omission

A balance on the ledger account is omitted from the trial balance.

Example (vi)

The discounts received balance of £350 was unintentionally excluded from the trial balance. The corresponding debit balance was correctly included in the general ledger.

What was the original entry?

Account name	Debit £	Credit £
Discounts received in the TB		0
Suspense β		350

What should the entry have been?

Account name	Debit £	Credit £
Discount received in the TB		350

Prepare journal entries to:

(a) Record the correct entry

Account name	Debit £	Credit £
Discount received in the TB		350

(b) Remove the suspense account balance

Account name	Debit £	Credit £
Suspense	350	

Transposition error

The digits in a number are transposed (swapped round) in:

- One general ledger account (eg debit entry); or
- The balance on a general ledger account when it is taken to the trial balance.

Note that if a transposition error has occurred, the difference between total debits and total credits is exactly divisible by nine. This is a useful trick to know when identifying errors.

Example (vii)

A purchases return is recorded correctly in the payables ledger control account as £402 but incorrectly in purchases returns as £420.

What was the original entry?

Account name	Debit £	Credit £
Payables ledger control	402	
Purchases returns		420
Suspense β	18	

What should the entry have been?

Account name	Debit £	Credit £
Payables ledger control	402	
Purchases returns		402

Prepare journal entries to:

(a) Remove the incorrect entry

Account name	Debit	Credit
	£	£
Purchases returns	420	

(b) Record the correct entry

Account name	Debit	Credit
	£	£
Purchases returns		402

(c) Remove the suspense account balance

Account name	Debit	Credit
	£	£
Suspense		18

The suspense account will be cleared by posting the journals to correct the errors which refer to the suspense account:

Suspense

Details	Amount	Details	Amount
	£		£
Balance b/f	9,500	Wages and salaries expense (i)	4,482
Bank (iii)	100	Electricity expense (ii)	5,000
Petty cash account in the TB (v)	50	Receivables ledger control (iv)	500
Discounts received in the TB (vi)	350	Purchases returns (vii)	18
	10,000		10,000

The suspense account now stands at nil as there is no balance c/d after the relevant entries have been made. This shows that the errors have been corrected. A redrafted trial balance could now be prepared.

3 Errors and the trial balance

It is important to understand the types of errors that are disclosed by the trial balance and those that are not. We will test your knowledge of this topic in the next activity.

As you are working through this example, consider the trial balance totals. Will the error you are addressing cause an imbalance in the totals?

Activity 1: Errors and the trial balance

Show which of the errors below are, or are not, disclosed by the trial balance.

Error in the general ledger	Error disclosed by the trial balance ✓	Error NOT disclosed by the trial balance ✓
Recording a receipt of bank interest on the debit side of both the bank and bank interest accounts		
Recording a payment for a motor vehicle in the motor expenses account		
Recording a purchases credit note on the credit side of the payables ledger control account and the debit side of the purchases returns account		
Incorrectly calculating the balance on the wages and salaries account		
Recording a receipt by cheque from a customer in the bank account and receivables ledger only		
Recording a bank payment of £510 for electricity as £5,100 in both accounts		

4 Opening a suspense account

If an initial trial balance does not balance, you may need to open a suspense account. The steps are:

(a) Find the difference between the total of the debit and total of the credit columns

(b) Include the difference in the column with the lower (draft) total, so that if you were preparing a trial balance the two sides balance.

Activity 2: Opening a suspense account

Bee's trial balance was extracted and did not balance. The debit column of the trial balance totalled £390,200 and the credit column totalled £380,400.

Required

What entry would be made in the suspense account to balance the trial balance?

Account name	Amount £	Debit ✓	Credit ✓
Suspense			

5 Identifying and correcting errors

Remember, the steps to follow to identify and correct errors are to:

- Identify what the incorrect double entry was
- Determine what the correct double entry should have been
- Prepare the journal entries to:
  - Remove the incorrect entry

- Record the correct entry
- Remove the suspense account balance

Activity 3: Identifying and correcting errors

Julian's initial trial balance includes a suspense account with a balance of £150.

The error has been traced to the sales returns day book shown below.

Sales returns day book

Date	Details	Credit note number	Total	VAT	Net
20XX			£	£	£
31 Jan	Brian	208	672	112	560
31 Jan	Elsie	209	4,200	700	3,500
31 Jan	Simon	210	3,384	564	2,820
	Totals		8,256	1,526	6,880

Note – (a) and (b) are preparation workings for (c) and do not form part of an exam standard answer.

Required

(a) What was the original entry?

Account name	Amount	Debit	Credit
	£	✓	✓

(b) What should the entry have been?

Account name	Amount	Debit	Credit
	£	✓	✓

(c) Identify the error and record the journal entries needed in the general ledger to:

(1) Remove the incorrect entry

(2) Record the correct entry

(3) Remove the suspense account balance

Journal entries:

(1) Remove the incorrect entry

Account name		Amount	Debit	Credit
		£	✓	✓
▼				

(2)   Record the correct entry

Account name		Amount	Debit	Credit
		£	✓	✓
▼				

(3)   Remove the suspense account balance

Account name		Amount	Debit	Credit
		£	✓	✓
▼				

Picklist

- Brian
- Elsie
- Payables ledger control
- Purchases
- Purchases returns
- Receivables ledger control
- Sales
- Sales returns
- Simon
- Suspense
- VAT

An entry to record a bank receipt from a credit customer for £4,400 has been reversed.

Required

(d) Record the journal entries needed in the general ledger to:

(1) Remove the incorrect entry

(2) Record the correct entry

Journal entries:

(1)   Remove the incorrect entry

Account name		Amount	Debit	Credit
		£	✓	✓
▼				
▼				

(2)   Record the correct entry

Account name		Amount	Debit	Credit
		£	✓	✓
▼				
▼				

Picklist

- Bank
- Cash
- Payables ledger control
- Purchases
- Receivables ledger control
- Sales
- Suspense
- VAT

Assessment focus point

In the assessment you may well be asked to record the journal entry to open a suspense account so that an initial trial balance balances. You will also be asked to record the journal entries to remove any incorrect entries and record the correct entries. This may include posting a journal entry to remove a suspense account balance.

6 Posting journals to correct errors

Once the bookkeeper has noted the journals needed to correct errors in the accounting records, the journals need to be posted to the general ledger.

Here, you need to work down the list of journals, posting them to the relevant general ledger account. Remember to include each entry on the correct side of the ledger accounts and cross-reference them appropriately.

Where there is a suspense account, once all the journal entries have been posted, the suspense account will stand at 'nil'.

Activity 4: Posting journals to the general ledger

The journal entries below have been prepared to correct errors.

Journal entries

Account name	Debit	Credit
	£	£
Telephone	242	
Suspense		242
Suspense	2,200	

Account name	Debit	Credit
	£	£
Purchases		2,200

Required

Post the journal entries to the general ledger accounts below. Total the accounts. Show the balance carried down in the telephone and purchase accounts.

Telephone

Details	Amount	Details	Amount
	£		£
Balance b/f	1,872	▼	
Bank	550	▼	
▼		▼	

Purchases

Details	Amount	Details	Amount
	£		£
Balance b/f	4,300	▼	
Payables ledger control	11,100	▼	

Suspense

Details	Amount	Details	Amount
	£		£
▼		Balance b/f	1,958
▼		▼	

Picklist

- Balance b/f
- Balance c/d
- Purchases
- Suspense
- Telephone

Redrafting the trial balance following the correction of errors

Earlier in the chapter we looked at opening a suspense account, to balance an initial trial balance.

When you are redrafting a trial balance following the correction of errors, the steps are as follows:

(a) Review the journal entries and note the balances that will change as a result of the journal entries.

(b) Enter the unaffected numbers into the trial balance.

(c) Process the journals given in the scenario. (You will need to do this on scrap paper and may like to set up T-accounts to do this.) Once the journals are posted include the revised numbers in the trial balance.

(d) Total the trial balance and include the totals in the debit and credit columns.

(e) As a check that you have posted the entries correctly, the columns should now balance.

Activity 5: Redrafting the trial balance following the correction of errors

On 30 September, Molly Co extracted an initial trial balance which did not balance, and a suspense account was opened with a £18,874 debit balance. On 1 October journal entries were prepared to correct the errors that had been found, and clear the suspense account. The list of balances in the initial trial balance, and the journal entries to correct the errors, are shown below.

Journal entries

Account name	Debit £	Credit £
Bank	9,482	
Suspense		9,482
Bank	9,482	
Suspense		9,482

Account name	Debit £	Credit £
Purchases returns	2,431	
Suspense		2,431
Purchases returns		2,521
Suspense	2,521	

Required

Redraft the trial balance by placing the figures in the debit or credit column. You should take into account the journal entries that will clear the suspense account.

Account names	Balances extracted on 30 September £	Balances at 1 October Debit £	Credit £
Plant	54,824		
Equipment	28,424		
Inventory	15,392		
Bank (overdraft)	9,482		
Petty cash	200		

Account names	Balances extracted on 30 September	Balances at 1 October	
		Debit	Credit
	£	£	£
Receivables ledger control	64,136		
Payables ledger control	65,024		
VAT owing to HM Revenue & Customs	9,424		
Capital	20,000		
Sales	309,565		
Purchases	140,592		
Purchases returns	2,431		
Wages	75,302		
Motor expenses	504		
Office expenses	6,825		
Rent and rates	4,265		
Heat and light	1,100		
Insurance	247		
Miscellaneous expenses	5,241		
Totals			

Chapter summary

- Errors in the accounting records that do not cause an imbalance on the trial balance are:
  - Error of original entry
  - Error of omission
  - Error of commission
  - Error of principle
  - Reversal of entries
  - Compensating error.
- Once identified, draft journal entries to (i) reverse the incorrect entries and (ii) make the correct entries.
- Some errors in the accounting records cause an imbalance on the trial balance – these include:
  - Single entry transactions
  - Two debits/two credits
  - Unequal amounts error
  - Calculation error
  - Balance transfer error
  - Balance omission
  - Transposition error.
- If the trial balance does not balance, set up a suspense account to make the debits equal to the credits.
- Once the errors have been found, for each one:
  - Identify what the incorrect double entry was
  - Determine what the correct double entry should have been
  - Prepare the journal entries to:
  - Remove the incorrect entry
  - Record the correct entry
  - Remove the suspense account balance
  - Redraft the trial balance (where required).

Activity answers

Activity 1: Errors and the trial balance

The correct answers are:

Error in the general ledger	Error disclosed by the trial balance ✓	Error NOT disclosed by the trial balance ✓
Recording a receipt of bank interest on the debit side of both the bank and bank interest accounts	✓	
Recording a payment for a motor vehicle in the motor expenses account		✓
Recording a purchases credit note on the credit side of the payables ledger control account and the debit side of the purchases returns account		✓
Incorrectly calculating the balance on the wages and salaries account	✓	
Recording a receipt by cheque from a customer in the bank account and receivables ledger only	✓	
Recording a bank payment of £510 for electricity as £5,100 in both accounts		✓

Although items 2, 3 and 6 are recorded incorrectly, both sides of the entries are for the same amount and therefore will not cause an imbalance in the trial balance.

However, item 1 is a two debit entry; as there is no corresponding credit entry, the trial balance will not balance. Likewise, in item 4 the balance on the wages and salaries account is incorrect; the corresponding entries will be for the correct amount, and hence the difference leading to an imbalance in the trial balance.

For item 5 the debit entry for the bank receipt has been recorded in the general ledger but the credit entry has not been posted to the receivables ledger control account; hence an imbalance. The entry to the subsidiary receivables ledger does not affect the trial balance.

Activity 2: Opening a suspense account

Account name	Amount £	Debit ✓	Credit ✓
Suspense	9,800		✓

In the initial trial balance the debit column total exceeds the credit column total by £9,800. Therefore, to temporarily balance the trial balance, a suspense account with a credit of £9,800 is opened.

Activity 3: Identifying and correcting errors

(a) What was the original entry?

Account name	Amount £	Debit ✓	Credit ✓
Sales returns	6,880	✓	
VAT	1,526	✓	
Receivables ledger control	8,256		✓
Suspense	150		✓

(b) What should the entry have been?

Account name	Amount £	Debit ✓	Credit ✓
Sales returns	6,880	✓	
VAT	1,376	✓	
Receivables ledger control	8,256		✓

(c) Journal entries:

(1) Remove the incorrect entry

Account name	Amount £	Debit ✓	Credit ✓
VAT	1,526		✓

(2) Record the correct entry

Account name	Amount £	Debit ✓	Credit ✓
VAT	1,376	✓	

(3) Remove the suspense account balance

Account name	Amount £	Debit ✓	Credit ✓
Suspense	150	✓	

(d) Journal entries:

(1) Remove the incorrect entry

Account name	Amount £	Debit ✓	Credit ✓
Bank	4,400	✓	
Receivables ledger control	4,400		✓

(2) Record the correct entry

Account name	Amount	Debit	Credit
	£	✓	✓
Bank	4,400	✓	
Receivables ledger control	4,400		✓

Activity 4: Posting journals to the general ledger

Telephone

Details	Amount	Details	Amount
	£		£
Balance b/f	1,872	Balance c/d	2,664
Bank	550		
Suspense	242		
	2,664		2,664

Purchases

Details	Amount	Details	Amount
	£		£
Balance b/f	4,300	Suspense	2,200
Payables ledger control	11,100	Balance c/d	13,200
	15,400		15,400

Suspense

Details	Amount	Details	Amount
	£		£
Purchases	2,200	Balance b/f	1,958
		Telephone	242
	2,200		2,200

To post the journal entries work methodically down the list of debit and credit items given in the scenario. Ensure that you cross-reference them accurately between the T-accounts. For example, the debit in the telephone T-account of £242 must be cross-referenced to the credit in the suspense account of £242.

Activity 5: Redrafting the trial balance following the correction of errors

Account names	Balances extracted on 30 September	Balances at 1 October	
		Debit	Credit
	£	£	£
Plant	54,824	58,824	

Account names	Balances extracted on 30 September	Balances at 1 October	
		Debit	Credit
	£	£	£
Equipment	28,424	28,424	
Inventory	15,392	15,392	
Bank (overdraft)	9,482	**9,482**	
Petty cash	200	200	
Receivables ledger control	64,136	64,136	
Payables ledger control	65,024		65,024
VAT owing to HM Revenue & Customs	9,424		9,424
Capital	20,000		20,000
Sales	309,565		309,565
Purchases	140,592	140,592	
Purchases returns	2,431		**2,521**
Wages	75,302	75,302	
Motor expenses	504	504	
Office expenses	6,825	6,825	
Rent and rates	4,265	4,265	
Heat and light	1,100	1,100	
Insurance	247	247	
Miscellaneous expenses	5,241	5,241	
Totals		406,534	406,534

> **Tutorial note.** The journal entries to the suspense, bank and purchases returns accounts are as follows:

Suspense account

Details	Amount	Details	Amount
	£		£
Balance b/d in the initial trial balance	18,874	Bank (to remove error to bank)	9,482
Purchases returns (to correctly include purchases returns)	2,521	Bank (to correctly include bank)	9,482
		Purchases returns (to remove error to purchases returns)	2,431
	21,395		21,395

Bank

Details	Amount £	Details	Amount £
Suspense (to remove error to bank)	9,482	Balance b/d in the initial trial balance	9,482
Suspense (to correctly include bank)	9,482	Balance c/d in the redrafted trial balance	9,482
	18,964		18,964
Balance b/d in the redrafted trial balance	9,482		

Purchases returns

Details	Amount £	Details	Amount £
Suspense (to remove error to purchases returns)	2,431	Balance b/d in the initial trial balance	2,431
Balance c/d in the redrafted trial balance	2,521	Suspense (to correctly include purchases returns)	2,521
	4,952		4,952
		Balance b/d in the redrafted trial balance	2,521

Test your learning

1 It is important to understand the types of error that are disclosed by the trial balance and those that are not.

Required

Show which of the errors below are, or are not, disclosed by the trial balance.

Error in the general ledger	Error disclosed by the trial balance ✓	Error NOT disclosed by the trial balance ✓
Calculating the balance on a ledger account incorrectly by £100		
Recording a supplier's credit note for £800 at £80 in the purchases returns day book		
Forgetting to include a £200 balance for motor expenses in the trial balance		
Making the debit entry for a cash sale of £150 but not the credit entry		
Forgetting to record a petty cash payment of £20		
For a purchase of stationery on credit, debiting the PLCA and crediting the stationery account		

2 Alvescot Co's trial balance was extracted and did not balance. The debit column of the trial balance totalled £52,673 and the credit column totalled £61,920.

Required

What entry would be made in the suspense account to balance the trial balance?

Account name	Amount £	Debit ✓	Credit ✓
Suspense			

3 An initial trial balance has a credit balance on the suspense account of £900. It was found that a receipt of £3,250 from a customer was recorded in the cash book correctly but in the receivables ledger control account as £2,350.

Required

Using the picklist, record the journal entries needed in the general ledger to:

(1) Remove the amount entered incorrectly

(2) Record the correct entry

(3) Remove the suspense account balance

Journal entries:

(1) Remove the amount entered incorrectly

Account name	Amount £	Debit ✓	Credit ✓
▼			

(2) Record the correct entry

Account name	Amount £	Debit ✓	Credit ✓
▼			

(3) Remove the suspense account balance

Account name	Amount £	Debit ✓	Credit ✓
▼			

Picklist

- Bank
- Receivables ledger control
- Suspense

4 The initial trial balance of a business includes a suspense account with a balance of £1,000.

The error has been traced to the casting of the net column of the purchases day book shown below.

Purchases day book

Date20XX	Details	Invoice number	Total	VAT	Net
20XX			£	£	£
31 Oct	Hughson Ltd	1902	1,740	290	1,450
31 Oct	Rundle Co	43902	432	72	360
31 Oct	Westcot Jenks	6327	2,562	427	2,135
	Totals		4,734	789	4,945

Required

(a) Record the journal entries needed in the general ledger to:

(1) **Remove the amount entered incorrectly**

(2) **Record the correct entry**

(3) **Remove the suspense account balance**

Journal entries:

(1) Remove the amount entered incorrectly

Account name		Amount £	Debit ✓	Credit ✓
▼				

(2) Record the correct entry

Account name		Amount £	Debit ✓	Credit ✓
▼				

(3) Remove the suspense account balance

Account name		Amount £	Debit ✓	Credit ✓
▼				

Picklist

- Payables ledger control
- Purchases
- Suspense

(b) An entry to record purchases of goods on credit for £980 (no VAT) has been reversed. Using the picklist, record the journal entries needed in the general ledger to:

(1) Remove the incorrect entries

(2) Record the correct entries

Journal entries:

(1) Remove the incorrect entries

Account name		Amount £	Debit ✓	Credit ✓
▼				
▼				

(2) Record the correct entries

Account name		Amount £	Debit ✓	Credit ✓
▼				
▼				

Picklist

- Bank
- Payables ledger control
- Purchases

5 The initial trial balance of a business included a suspense account. All the bookkeeping errors have now been traced and the journal entries shown below have been recorded.

Journal entries

Account name	Debit £	Credit £
Discounts allowed	149	
Discounts received		149
Suspense	256	
Purchases		256
Motor expenses	893	
Suspense		893

Required

Post the journal entries to the general ledger accounts.

Purchases

Details	Amount £	Details	Amount £
▼		▼	
▼		▼	

Motor expenses

Details	Amount £	Details	Amount £
▼		▼	
▼		▼	

Suspense

Details	Amount £	Details	Amount £
Balance b/f	637	▼	
▼		▼	

Discounts received

Details	Amount £	Details	Amount £
▼		▼	

Details	Amount £	Details	Amount £
▼		▼	

Discounts allowed

Details	Amount £	Details	Amount £
▼		▼	
▼		▼	

Picklist

- Balance b/f
- Discounts allowed
- Discounts received
- Motor expenses
- Purchases
- Suspense

Test your learning answers

Chapter 1

1 The correct answers are:

	True ✓	False ✓
A bank draft cannot be cancelled once it has been issued.	✓	
Any customer who pays with a debit card is taking out a loan with their bank as a result.		✓

2

Statement	Impact on bank account
When a payment is made using a debit card, the money leaves the bank account	immediately
When a payment is made using a credit card, the money leaves the bank account	at a later date

3

Statement	Impact on bank account
When a payment is made using BACS direct credit, the money leaves the bank account	immediately
When a payment is made using CHAPS, the money leaves the bank account	immediately

4

Statement	Term
In respect of cheques, the person to whom the cheque is payable is the	payee
In respect of cheques, the person writing and signing the cheque in order to make the payment is the	drawer
In respect of cheques, the bank which has issued the cheque and will have to pay the cheque (ie the customer's bank) is the	drawee

5 A standing order is a method of making the same regular payment for a fixed amount directly from a business's bank account to the bank account of a supplier.

Chapter 2

1 The correct answer is:

	✓
A debit entry	
A credit entry	✓

2 The correct answer is:

	✓
Debit side of the cash book	✓
Credit side of the cash book	

3 The correct answer is:

	✓
Debit side of the cash book	
Credit side of the cash book	✓

4 The correct answer is:

	✓
As an unpresented cheque	✓
As an outstanding lodgement	

5 **Cash book**

Date	Details	Bank	Date	Cheque number	Details	Bank
20XX		£	20XX			£
01 Feb	Balance b/f	6,230	01 Feb	003252	Jeggers Ltd	2,567
20 Feb	Straightens Co	2,228	01 Feb	003253	Short & Fell	333
21 Feb	Plumpers	925	01 Feb	003254	Rastop Ltd	1,006
22 Feb	Eastern Supplies	1,743	01 Feb	003255	A & D Trading	966
09 Feb	Branthill Co	1,559	02 Feb	003256	Jesmond Warr	2,309
			02 Feb	003257	Nistral Ltd	3,775
			13 Feb	003258	Simpsons	449
			13 Feb		AxDC	250

Date	Details	Bank	Date	Cheque number	Details	Bank
20XX		£	20XX			£
			18 Feb		DD Trust Insurance	325
			20 Feb		Bank charges	14
			22 Feb		Interest charge	56
			23 Feb		Balance c/d	635
		12,685				12,685
24 Feb	Balance b/d	635				

Bank reconciliation statement as at 23 February 20XX

Bank reconciliation statement	£
Balance per bank statement	725
Add:	
Pumpers	925
Eastern Supplies	1,743
Total to add	2,668
Less:	
Jesmond Warr	2,309
Simpsons	449
Total to subtract	2,758
Balance as per cash book	635

Chapter 3

1

Account name	Amount	Debit	Credit
	£	✓	✓
Sales returns	1,500	✓	
VAT	300	✓	
Receivables ledger control	1,800		✓

 BPP

2

Account name	Amount	Debit	Credit
	£	✓	✓
Payables ledger control	900	✓	
VAT	150		✓
Purchases returns	750		✓

3 General ledger

Receivables ledger control

Details	Amount	Details	Amount
	£		£
Balance b/d	780.31	Bank	670.11
Sales	906.24	Balance c/d	1,016.44
	1,686.55		1,686.55
Balance b/d	1,016.44		

Receivables ledger
Virgo Partners

Details	Amount	Details	Amount
	£		£
Balance b/d	227.58	Bank	117.38
Invoice	96.72		
Invoice	214.44	Balance c/d	421.36
	538.74		538.74
Balance b/d	421.36		

McGowan & Sons

Details	Amount	Details	Amount
	£		£
Balance b/d	552.73	Bank	552.73
Invoice	595.08	Balance c/d	595.08
	1,147.81		1,147.81
Balance b/d	595.08		

Reconciliation

	Amount £
Receivables ledger control account balance as at 31 May	1,016.44
Total of receivables ledger accounts as at 31 May	1,016.44
Difference	0

Working

	Amount £
Virgo Partners	421.36
McGowan & Sons	595.08
Total	1,016.44

4 General ledger

Payables ledger control

Details	Amount £	Details	Amount £
Bank	744.68	Balance b/d	591.56
Balance c/d	824.40	Purchases	977.52
	1,569.08		1,569.08
		Balance b/d	824.40

Payables ledger
Jenkins Suppliers

Details	Amount £	Details	Amount £
Bank	441.56	Balance b/d	441.56
Balance c/d	671.28	Invoice	219.96
		Invoice	451.32
	1,112.84		1,112.84
		Balance b/d	671.28

Kilnfarm Paper

Details	Amount £	Details	Amount £
Bank	150.00	Balance b/d	150.00
Bank	153.12	Invoice	153.12

 BPP

Details	Amount £	Details	Amount £
Balance c/d	153.12	Invoice	153.12
	456.24		456.24
		Balance b/d	153.12

Reconciliation

	£
Payables ledger control account balance as at 31 May	824.40
Total of payables ledger accounts as at 31 May	824.40
Difference	0

Working

	£
Jenkins Suppliers	671.28
Kilnfarm Paper	153.12
Total	824.40

5 (a) VAT control

	Amount £		Amount £
Purchases	14,368	Sales	29,072
Sales returns	858	Cash sales	332
		Purchases returns	488

(b) The correct answer is:

	✓
Yes	
No	✓

The amount is owing **to** HMRC, not from HMRC. The total credits exceed the debits and therefore there is a liability.

Chapter 4

1 The correct answers are:

Statement	True ✓	False ✓
An aged receivables analysis is a schedule showing, for each credit customer, how long the component parts of the balance have been unpaid.	✓	

2 The correct answer is:

	✓
The sales day book was undercast by £250 on one page.	
An invoice for £250 was omitted from the receivables ledger account.	✓
A discount allowed to a customer of £250 was posted to the debit side of the receivables ledger account.	
Cash received of £250 was only posted to the receivables ledger control account.	

Per the scenario, the receivables ledger control account balance is higher than the total of the receivables ledger account balances, and therefore:

Statement 1 – this cannot be correct. In the event that the sales day book totals are undercast, the receivables ledger control account would be lower than the total of the receivables ledger balances.

Statement 2 – this is correct as a debit balance of £250 has been omitted from the receivables ledger; therefore it is lower than the control account by this amount.

Statement 3 – this is incorrect as debit entries increase the receivables ledger balances; therefore, if a discount allowed was posted to the debit side of the receivables ledger account (but correctly entered in the control account), the receivables ledger totals would be higher than the control account balance.

Statement 4 – this is incorrect. If cash received is only omitted from the receivables ledgers, the total of the ledger balances will be higher than the control account balance.

3

Account name	Amount £	Debit ✓	Credit ✓
Irrecoverable debt expenses	1,200	✓	
VAT	240	✓	
Receivables ledger control	1,440		✓

4

Account name	Amount £	Debit ✓	Credit ✓
Irrecoverable debts	1,290	✓	
VAT	258	✓	
Receivables ledger control	1,548		✓

5 (a)

Details	Amount £	Debit ✓	Credit ✓
Amount due to credit suppliers at 1 August	42,394		✓
Payments to credit suppliers	39,876	✓	
Purchases on credit	31,243		✓
Purchases returned to credit suppliers	1,266	✓	
Discounts received	501	✓	

(b) The correct answer is:

	✓
Debit £31,994	
Credit £31,994	✓
Debit £34,526	
Credit £34,526	
Debit £32,996	
Credit £32,996	

(c)

	Amount £
Payables ledger control account balance as at 31 August	31,994
Total of payables ledger accounts as at 31 August	32,190
Difference	196

(d) The correct answer is:

	✓
A debit balance in the payables ledger may have been included as a credit balance when calculating the total of the list of balances.	✓
A credit balance in the payables ledger may have been included as a debit balance when calculating the total of the list of balances.	
A credit note may have been omitted from the purchase returns day book total.	
Discounts received may only have been entered in the payables ledger.	

The total of the subsidiary payables ledger accounts exceeds the payables ledger control account balance by £196.

 BPP

Statement 1 – in the payables ledger, credit entries increase the closing balance. Therefore, including a debit balance as a credit balance explains the difference.

Statement 2 – including a credit balance as a debit balance in the payables ledger would result in the total of the payables ledger account balances being lower than the payables ledger control account balance, and therefore this statement is incorrect.

Statements 3 and 4 – omitting credit note and discount received balances from the payables ledger control account would result in the payables ledger control account balance being higher than the total of the subsidiary payables ledger accounts. This is not the case and therefore these statements are incorrect.

Chapter 5

1

Account name	Amount £	Debit ✓	Credit ✓
Capital	28,000		✓
Cash at bank	21,000	✓	
Loan from bank	5,000		✓
Machinery	12,000	✓	

2 £ 1,642.84

Working

	Amount £
Gross pay (£27,000/12)	2,250.00
Income tax	(418.16)
Employee's NIC	(189.00)
Net pay	1,642.84

3 The correct answers are:

	Statutory deduction ✓	Voluntary deduction ✓
Pension contributions		✓
Income tax	✓	
Employee's NIC	✓	
Trade union fees		✓

4   The correct answers are:

	True ✓	False ✓
Employer's NIC are deducted from gross pay.		✓
Employer's pension contributions are in addition to gross pay.	✓	

5   (a)

Account name	Amount £	Debit ✓	Credit ✓
Wages expense	13,766	✓	
Wages control	13,766		✓

Working

£12,756 + £1,020 = £13,776

(b)

Account name	Amount £	Debit ✓	Credit ✓
Wages control	3,698	✓	
HM Revenue and Customs	3,698		✓

Working

£1,020 + £765 + £1,913 = £3,698

(c)

Account name	Amount £	Debit ✓	Credit ✓
Wages control	9,978	✓	
Bank	9,978		✓

Working

£12,756 − £1,913 − £765 − £100 = £9,978

(d)

Account name	Amount £	Debit ✓	Credit ✓
Wages control	100	✓	
Trade union liability	100		✓

Chapter 6

1 VAT account

Details	Amount £	Details	Amount £
Purchases	3,778	Balance b/f	2,116
Bank	2,116	Sales	6,145
Balance c/d	2,367		
	8,261		8,261
		Balance b/d	2,367

Sales

Details	Amount £	Details	Amount £
		Balance b/f	57,226
Balance c/d	100,121	Receivables ledger control	42,895
	100,121		100,121
		Balance b/d	100,121

Receivables ledger control

Details	Amount £	Details	Amount £
Balance b/f	4,689	Bank	21,505
Sales	23,512	Discounts allowed	2,019
		Balance c/d	4,677
	28,201		28,201
Balance b/d	4,677		

Payables ledger control

Details	Amount £	Details	Amount £
Purchase returns	1,334	Balance b/f	2,864
Bank	13,446	Purchases	14,552
Discounts received	662		
Balance c/d	1,974		
	17,416		17,416
		Balance b/d	1,974

2

	Amount	Debit balance	Credit balance
	£	✓	✓
Discounts allowed	1,335	✓	
Discounts received	1,013		✓
Purchase returns	4,175		✓
Sales returns	6,078	✓	
Bank interest received	328		✓
Bank charges	163	✓	

3

		Debit	Credit
	£	£	£
Motor vehicles	64,000	64,000	
Office equipment	21,200	21,200	
Sales	238,000		238,000
Purchases	164,000	164,000	
Cash	300	300	
Bank overdraft	1,080		1,080
Petty cash	30	30	
Capital	55,000		55,000
Sales returns	4,700	4,700	
Purchase returns	3,600		3,600
Receivables ledger control	35,500	35,500	
Payables ledger control	30,100		30,100
VAT (owed to HMRC)	12,950		12,950
Telephone	1,600	1,600	
Electricity	2,800	2,800	
Wages	62,100	62,100	
Loan from bank	30,000		30,000
Discounts allowed	6,400	6,400	
Discounts received	3,900		3,900
Rent expense	12,000	12,000	
Totals		374,630	374,630

 BPP

4

Account name	Amount £	Debit £	Credit £
Advertising	3,238	3,238	
Bank overdraft	27,511		27,511
Capital	40,846		40,846
Cash	689	689	
Discount allowed	4,416	4,416	
Discount received	2,880		2,880
Hotel expenses	2,938	2,938	
Inventory	46,668	46,668	
Loan from bank	39,600		39,600
Miscellaneous expenses	3,989	3,989	
Motor expenses	7,087	7,087	
Motor vehicles	63,120	63,120	
Payables ledger control	110,846		110,846
Petty cash	720	720	
Purchases	634,529	634,529	
Purchase returns	1,618		1,618
Receivables ledger control	405,000	405,000	
Rent and rates	19,200	19,200	
Sales	1,051,687		1,051,687
Sales returns	11,184	11,184	
Stationery	5,880	5,880	
Subscriptions	864	864	
Telephone	3,838	3,838	
VAT (owing to HMRC)	63,650		63,650
Wages	125,278	125,278	
Totals		1,338,638	1,338,638

5 Trial balance

Account name	Amount £	Debit £	Credit £
Cash	520.00	520.00	

Account name	Amount £	Debit £	Credit £
Bank	9,320.00	9,320.00	
Receivables ledger control	10,000.00	10,000.00	
Sales	21,650.00		21,650.00
Sales returns	230.00	230.00	
VAT	640.00		640.00
Discounts allowed	40.00	40.00	
Payables ledger control	2,500.00		2,500.00
Purchases	6,300.00	6,300.00	
Purchase returns	480.00		480.00
Discounts received	140.00		140.00
Capital	1,000.00		1,000.00
		26,410.00	26,410.00

Chapter 7

1 The correct answers are:

Error in the general ledger	Error disclosed by the trial balance ✓	Error NOT disclosed by the trial balance ✓
Calculating the balance on a ledger account incorrectly by £100	✓	
Recording a supplier's credit note for £800 at £80 in the purchases returns day book		✓
Forgetting to include a £200 balance for motor expenses in the trial balance	✓	
Making the debit entry for a cash sale of £150 but not the credit entry	✓	
Forgetting to record a petty cash payment of £20		✓
For a purchase of stationery on credit, debiting the PLCA and crediting the stationery account		✓

Statement 1 – the debit and credit entries differ by £100; this will be disclosed by the trial balance

Statement 2 – the amount is incorrect; however, the amount posted is the same on the debit and credit sides and therefore this will not be disclosed by the trial balance

Statement 3 – the debit and credit column totals differ by £200 in respect of this transaction; therefore the trial balance will not balance

Statement 4 – only the debit entry relating to this cash sale has been posted; the credit entry has not been posted and therefore the trial balance will not balance

Statement 5 – the item is omittedand therefore the trial balance will still balance

Statement 6 – the debit and credit entries have been reversed and are therefore incorrect; however, they are equal and so the trial balance will still balance

2

Account name	Amount	Debit	Credit
	£	✓	✓
Suspense	9,247	✓	

3 Journal entries:

(1) Remove the amount entered incorrectly

Account name	Amount	Debit	Credit
	£	✓	✓
Receivables ledger control	2,350	✓	

(2) Record the correct entry

Account name	Amount	Debit	Credit
	£	✓	✓
Receivables ledger control	3,250		✓

(3) Remove the suspense account balance

Account name	Amount	Debit	Credit
	£	✓	✓
Suspense	900	✓	

4 (a) Journal entries:

(1) Remove the amount entered incorrectly

Account name	Amount	Debit	Credit
	£	✓	✓
Purchases	4,945		✓

(2) Record the correct entry

Account name	Amount	Debit	Credit
	£	✓	✓
Purchases	3,945	✓	

(3) Remove the suspense account balance

Account name	Amount £	Debit ✓	Credit ✓
Suspense	1,000	✓	

(b) Journal entries:

(1) Remove the incorrect entries

Account name	Amount £	Debit ✓	Credit ✓
Purchases	980	✓	
Payables ledger control	980		✓

(2) Record the correct entries

Account name	Amount £	Debit ✓	Credit ✓
Purchases	980	✓	
Payables ledger control	980		✓

5 Purchases

Details	Amount £	Details	Amount £
		Suspense	256

Motor expenses

Details	Amount £	Details	Amount £
Suspense	893		

Suspense

Details	Amount £	Details	Amount £
Balance b/f	637	Motor expenses	893
Purchases	256		

Discounts received

Details	Amount £	Details	Amount £
		Discounts allowed	149

Discounts allowed

Details	Amount £	Details	Amount £
Discounts received	149		

Synoptic assessment preparation

Certain *Principles of Bookkeeping Controls* assessment objectives will be tested in the AAT *Foundation Certificate in Accounting* synoptic assessment. Therefore, at this stage in your studies, it is useful to consider the style of tasks you may see in the synoptic assessment.

However, it is recommended that the AAT *Foundation Certificate in Accounting* synoptic assessment is only undertaken when all other units have been completed.

Question

This task is about control accounts, reconciliations and using journals to correct accounts.

One of your colleagues has expressed the view that there is no need for the business to keep control accounts, and that it would be better simply to post invoices directly to the general ledger instead.

You disagree, and believe that controls accounts serve an important purpose in the business.

Required

(a) State FOUR purposes of control accounts.

Kandinsky Ltd sells posters of images of artworks. The receivables ledger at 30 June shows the following balances are due from customers.

Customer name	Ref	Total £	VAT £	Net £
Art Worx Ltd	AW484	24,411.96	4,068.66	20,343.30
Person Art Co	PA120	20,219.88	3,369.98	16,849.90
Arty Gifts Co	AG243	14,217.84	2,369.64	11,848.20
The Painting Cupboard Ltd	PC223	9,431.16	1,571.86	7,859.30
Happy Shopper Co	HS545	6,773.16	1,128.86	5,644.30
Love Posters Ltd	LP003	5,152.44	858.74	4,293.70

Required

(b) If the receivables ledger control account and receivables ledger reconcile, what will be the debit balance? Enter your answer to two decimal places.

£ _____

The balance on the receivables ledger control account in the general ledger is a debit balance of £80,373.70.

Required

(c) What is the difference between the receivables ledger control account and the receivables ledger? Enter your answer to two decimal places.

£ ☐

(d) Identify whether or not the following statements could explain the difference between the two balances.

Reason	May explain the difference ✓	Does not explain the difference ✓
An error was made when casting the sales day book		
The gross amount of a sales invoice was posted incorrectly to the sales day book		

The cash book at the end of June shows a debit balance of £6,664.36. The following differences have been identified between the cash book and the balance per the bank statement:

- the bank statement includes some direct debits that are not included in the cash book
- these are an electricity direct debit of £374.24 and a phone direct debit of £134
- the cash book includes a cheque issued to a supplier for £2,400 two months ago. This is not included in the bank statement
- the bank has charged the business £24 in bank charges which are not in the cash book
- the cash book includes a customer receipt of £204. This was a cheque which was banked on 30 June but does not appear in the bank statement at that date.

Required

(e) Complete the adjustments to the cash book by selecting items from the picklist and entering figures in either the debit or credit column.

Cash book	Debit £	Credit £
Balance b/d before corrections	6,664.36	
▼		
▼		
Balance c/d after corrections		

Picklist

- Bank charges
- Cheque from customer
- Cheque to supplier
- Direct debits

Kandinsky Ltd has produced its year end trial balance and has identified the following error:

- a new printing press was purchased for long term use in the business. This has been debited to land and buildings.

 BPP

Required

(f) **Identify which type of error this is.**

	✓
Error of omission	
Error of commission	
Error of principle	
Compensating error	

(g) **Identify the impact on the suspense account of correcting this error.**

	✓
Debit	
Credit	
No effect	

Solution

(a) Answer should include four of these points.

- Control accounts contain summarised totals of all the individual transactions affecting their respective ledgers. They contain the same information as is in the receivables and payables accounts in the ledgers; however, they show the totals rather than the individual transactions.

- Transactions posted to the general ledger are kept to a minimum so there is less room for error in the general ledger double entry system.

- It is easy at any point in time to identify from the general ledger how much in total the business owes and is owed.

- The accuracy of the general ledger and the subsidiary ledgers can be checked by reconciling the balance on the control account in the former to the total of the balances on the latter.

- Performing reconciliations with the subsidiary ledgers prompts the business to identify and deal with discrepancies quickly.

- Segregation of duties is promoted within the organisation as one person could maintain the receivables and payables ledger accounts and another person could maintain the control accounts. This reduces the risk of fraud.

(b) £ 80,206.44

This is the total of all of the gross balances, given in the 'Total' column of the receivables ledger:

= 24,411.96 + 20,219.88 + 14,217.84 + 9,431.16 + 6,773.16 + 5,152.44

= 80,206.44

(c) £ 167.26

The total of the balances per the receivables ledger was £80,206.52. The difference between the receivables ledger and the receivables ledger control account is therefore:

= 80,373.70 − 80,206.44

= 167.26

(d) The correct answers are:

Reason	May explain the difference ✓	Does not explain the difference ✓
An error was made when casting the sales day book	✓	
The gross amount of a sales invoice was posted incorrectly to the sales day book		✓

If an error were made when casting the sales day book account then this could affect the amounts posted to the receivables ledger control account. This is due to the fact that the totals of the sales daybook are posted to the receivables ledger control account. It would not affect the receivables ledger balances, since these are derived from the individual rows of the sales day book. Hence the receivables ledger balances could differ from the control account balance.

If the gross amount of a sales invoice were posted incorrectly to the sales day book then this would affect the receivables ledger posting (which is from the invoice amount in the sales day book) and also the control account, which is posted from the totals in the same day book. Hence this would not explain the difference between the balances.

(e)

Cash book	Debit £	Credit £
Balance b/d before corrections	6,664.36	
Direct debits		508.24
Bank charges		24.00
Balance c/d after corrections		6,132.12

(f) The correct answer is:

	✓
Error of omission	
Error of commission	✓
Error of principle	
Compensating error	

This is an error of commission.

The amount should probably have been debited to plant and machinery, but since this land and buildings is the same class of account as plant and machinery (they are both non-current asset accounts) this is only an error of commission rather than an error of principle. This is not an error of omission because an entry was made into the accounting records, whereas an error of omission involves no entry being made at all. A compensating error describes a situation in which two errors are made and these cancel each other out, which is not the case here.

(g) The correct answer is:

	✓
Debit	
Credit	
No effect	✓

Correcting this error does not involve the suspense account because there was no imbalance between debits and credits. All that happened was that one entry was posted to the incorrect account, which does not affect the trial balance's ability to balance as such.

BPP

Glossary

Chapter 1: Payment methods

BACS (Bankers' Automated Clearing Services): This is an electronic system to make payments directly from one bank account to another. They are mainly used for direct debits and direct credits from organisations.

Bank statement: Shows payments into and out of the bank account since the date of the last bank statement and the closing balance on a certain date.

CHAPS: An instruction by the business to its bank to move a large amount of money to the recipient's account at another bank so the money is available the same working day.

Cheque: A customer's written order to their bank to pay a specified sum to a particular individual/organisation.

Clearing system: The system set up by the major banks to deal with the payment of cheques which means there is typically a delay of three business days between paying a cheque into an account and being able to access the money.

Credit card: A card that allows the customer to purchase goods and services on credit now but gives them flexibility as to when they repay the credit card company.

Debit card: A card that allows the customer to purchase goods and services where the sale is automatically debited from the customer's bank account and credited to the supplier's bank account.

Direct credit: A deposit of money by a payer directly into a payee's bank account.

Direct debit: A method of making payments direct from the bank where payments are for variable amounts and/or varying time intervals.

Dishonoured cheque: A cheque that has not been paid as expected by the bank on which it is drawn.

Faster payments: A system that allows customers to make small and medium-sized payments online almost instantaneously.

Paying-in slip: A pre-printed document for paying cash and cheques into a bank account.

Standing order: A method of making the same regular payment directly from a business's bank account to the bank account of a supplier or other third party.

Chapter 2: Bank reconciliations

Bank reconciliation statement: A statement reconciling the bank statement balance on a given date to the correct, adjusted cash book balance on the same date.

Outstanding lodgements: Cheques that have been received and recorded on the debit side of the cash book but do not yet appear on the bank statement.

Overdraft: This is where the business effectively owes the bank money – it appears as a debit balance in the bank statement and a credit balance in the cash book.

Timing differences: The reasons why the bank statement balance rarely agrees with the balance on the cash book, as receipts and payments recorded in the cash book appear later on the bank statement due to, for example, how the clearing system operates.

Unpresented cheques: Cheque payments that have been recorded in the credit side of the cash book but do not yet appear on the bank statement.

Chapter 3: Introduction to control accounts

Control account: A general ledger account that includes totals from the books of prime entry. This helps ensure that postings to the general ledger are complete and accurate.

Payables ledger control account: Totals for all the credit purchases transactions are posted to this account.

Payables ledger: Contains separate accounts for each credit supplier so that, at any time, a business knows how much it owes to each supplier.

Receivables ledger control account: Totals for all the credit sales transactions are posted to this account.

Receivables ledger: Contains separate accounts for each credit customer so that, at any time, a business knows how much it is owed by each customer.

Subsidiary ledgers: The receivables ledger and payables ledger, which contain a ledger account for each individual credit customer or credit supplier. They are not part of the general ledger.

VAT control account: Used for all transactions related to VAT, and allows the business to identify clearly how much is owed to HMRC in respect of VAT in a period, or how much is due from them.

Chapter 4: Preparing and reconciling control accounts

Aged trade receivables analysis: A schedule showing, for each credit customer, how long the component parts of the balance have been unpaid.

Irrecoverable debt: A debt which it is believed will never be recovered.

Payables ledger control account reconciliation: An exercise that agrees the balance on the payables ledger control account with the total of the list of balances in the payables ledger.

Receivables ledger control account reconciliation: An exercise that agrees the balance on the receivables ledger control account with the total of the list of balances in the receivables ledger.

Writing off: Removing an irrecoverable debt from the ledger accounts.

Chapter 5: The journal

Gross Pay: Gross pay is the salary or wages payable to an employee by the employer before any statutory or voluntary deductions.

His Majesty's Revenue and Customs (HMRC): The UK government department responsible for collecting tax.

Income tax: A tax that is paid by individuals on all sources of income, including salary/wages.

Journal book: The journal book is used to record transactions that do not appear in any of the other books of prime entry, so they can then be posted to the ledgers.

Journal entry: A written instruction to the bookkeeper to make a double entry into the ledgers.

National insurance contributions (employees' NIC): A tax on employees' income deducted from gross pay.

National insurance contributions (employer's NIC): An additional tax, suffered by the employer, based on an employee's gross pay.

Net pay: The amount of the employee's wages actually paid to the employee, net of statutory and voluntary deductions.

Payroll transactions: Payments to employees in respect of salaries and wages.

Pension contribution: A form of voluntary deduction from employees, and a contribution from employers which is paid to the pension administrator to provide a pension for the employee on retirement.

Statutory deductions: Deductions that must be made by the employer from an employee's pay in respect of income tax and employee's NIC.

Voluntary deductions: Non-statutory amounts deducted from employees' pay with their consent, eg give-as-you-earn (GAYE) and trade union subscriptions.

Wages control account: A control account for recording payroll transactions. This is like any other control account and helps ensure that the double entry is made correctly.

Chapter 6: Initial trial balance

Initial trial balance: A list of all the debit and credit balances brought down on the ledger accounts.

Chapter 7: Errors and the trial balance

Balance omission: A ledger account balance has been left out of the trial balance completely.

Balance transfer error: A balance on a general ledger account is transferred incorrectly into the trial balance.

Calculation error: A mistake is made in calculating the balance on a ledger account.

Compensating error: Two (or more) separate errors have been made that completely cancel each other out.

Error of commission: The double entry is arithmetically correct but one of the entries has been made to the wrong account, though an account of the correct type.

Error of omission: Both the debit and credit entries have been omitted from the ledger accounts.

Error of original entry: Both the debit and credit entries in the ledgers have been made at the wrong amount.

Error of principle: The double entry is arithmetically correct but one of the entries has been to the wrong type of account.

Reversal of entries: The debit and credit entries have been reversed in the ledger accounts.

Single entry transactions: Only one side of the double entry has been made.

Suspense account: An account opened in order to make the balances on a trial balance equal while the reason for the imbalance is discovered and corrected.

Transposition error: The digits in a number are transposed (swapped round).

Two debits/two credits error: Instead of a debit and a credit entry, either two debits or two credits have been made.

Unequal amounts error: Debit and credit entries have been made for different amounts.

 BPP

Index

Tell us what you think

Got comments or feedback on this book? Let us know.
Use your QR code reader:

Or, visit:
https://bppgroup.fra1.qualtrics.com/jfe/form/SV_9YwIGE0eqAS5G1E

Need to get in touch with customer service?

www.bpp.com/request-support

Spotted an error?

www.bpp.com/learningmedia/Errata